Mastering Taxation: A Comprehensive Guide to Tax Law and Practice

Welcome to "Mastering Taxation: A Comprehensive Guide to Tax Law and Practice." Taxation is an essential aspect of modern society, playing a vital role in funding government programs and services, shaping economic behavior, and promoting social welfare. For individuals, businesses, and governments alike, understanding the complexities of tax law is crucial in navigating the ever-evolving landscape of tax regulations and compliance.

This comprehensive guide aims to demystify the intricacies of tax law and provide readers with a deep understanding of tax principles, practices, and planning strategies. Whether you are a tax professional, a business owner, a law student, or an individual taxpayer, this book will serve as your invaluable companion in the world of taxation.

Through clear explanations, practical examples, and real-world scenarios, this book covers a wide range of topics, from the basics of income taxation and deductions to the complexities of international tax planning and compliance. You will explore various tax regimes, such as corporate tax, estate and gift tax, sales tax, and property tax, and gain insights into the latest developments and trends in tax policy.

Additionally, "Mastering Taxation" delves into the importance of ethical considerations in tax practice, the role of tax planning in optimizing financial decisions, and the impact of taxation on social justice and economic inequality. You will also find valuable guidance on navigating tax audits, resolving tax disputes, and maximizing tax benefits.

The ultimate goal of this book is to empower readers with the knowledge and tools needed to make informed decisions and comply with tax laws while ensuring that their financial and business endeavors are strategically aligned with their goals. We hope that this comprehensive guide will serve as a trusted resource in mastering the intricacies of taxation and enhance your ability to thrive in the ever-changing world of tax law and practice. Let's embark on this journey together as we explore the dynamic and critical field of taxation.

I. Introduction to Taxation

- Overview of Taxation and Its Significance
- Historical Development of Taxation
- Taxation and Social Policy

II. Foundations of Tax Law

- Constitutional Basis for Taxation
- Taxation Authorities and Agencies
- Tax Policy and Legislative Process
- Taxpayer Rights and Responsibilities

III. Individual Income Taxation

- Income Tax Basics and Filing Requirements
- Deductions, Exemptions, and Credits
- Tax Planning for Individuals
- Taxation of Investment Income
- Retirement Accounts and Taxation
- Taxation of Business Income for Sole Proprietors

IV. Corporate Taxation

- Corporate Tax Basics and Filing Requirements
- Tax Treatment of Business Expenses and Deductions
- Taxation of Corporate Distributions and Dividends
- International Tax Planning for Corporations
- Taxation of Pass-Through Entities (LLCs, Partnerships, etc.)

V. Estates & Trusts Taxation

- Estate Taxation and Filing Requirements
- Gift Taxation and Gift Tax Exclusions
- Taxation of Trusts and Trust Beneficiaries
- Estate Planning and Tax Minimization Strategies

VI. International Tax Law

- Principles of International Taxation
- Double Taxation Treaties and Tax Planning
- Controlled Foreign Corporations and Subpart F Rules
- Transfer Pricing and Base Erosion Profit Shifting (BEPS)
- Foreign Tax Credit and Foreign Earned Income Exclusion

VII. Sales & Use Tax

- Basics of Sales Tax and Nexus
- E-commerce and State Sales Tax Issues
- Use Tax and Reporting Requirements

VIII. Property Tax

- Assessment and Valuation of Real Property
- Property Tax Exemptions and Appeals

IX. Tax Audits and Disputes

- Tax Audits and IRS Examination Process
- Tax Litigation and Court Procedures
- Appeals and Taxpayer Representation

X. Tax Ethics and Professional Responsibility

- Ethics in Tax Practice
- Avoiding Tax Fraud and Abusive Tax Schemes

XI. Tax Policy and Social Justice

- Progressive Taxation and Economic Inequality
- Tax Incentives and Social Policy
- Taxation and Environmental Considerations

XII. Current Trends and Emerging Issues in Tax Law

- Digital Economy and Tax Challenges
- Cryptocurrency and Taxation
- Tax Implications of COVID-19 Relief Measures

XIII. Conclusion

Overview of Taxation and Its Significance

Taxation is the process of levying and collecting taxes on individuals, businesses, and other entities by the government to fund public services and meet various economic objectives. It is a fundamental aspect of any modern society and plays a crucial role in funding essential services, infrastructure development, and public welfare programs.

The significance of taxation can be understood through the following points:

1. Revenue Generation: Taxation is the primary source of revenue for governments at various levels - local, state, and federal. It provides funds to finance public services such as education, healthcare, infrastructure, law enforcement, and social welfare programs.

2. Economic Stabilization: Taxation can be used as an economic tool to influence consumer behavior and stimulate or restrain economic activities. For instance, governments may use tax incentives or penalties to promote investments, discourage certain practices, or control inflation.

3. Redistribution of Wealth: Progressive taxation, where higher-income individuals pay a higher percentage of their income as taxes, allows for income redistribution. This helps in reducing income inequality and providing financial assistance to low-income individuals and families.

4. Funding Government Operations: Taxes are essential for the functioning of government institutions, including the judiciary, legislature, and executive branches. They

support the operation and maintenance of these institutions.

5. Social and Environmental Objectives: Some taxes are designed to promote socially desirable behavior and environmental sustainability. For example, taxes on tobacco products aim to discourage smoking and promote public health.

6. Public Goods and Services: Taxation enables the provision of public goods and services that may not be feasible for the private sector to undertake. These include national defense, public parks, public schools, and emergency services.

7. Debt Reduction: Governments may use tax revenues to repay public debt and reduce budget deficits, contributing to overall economic stability.

8. Fiscal Policy Tool: Taxation is an integral part of fiscal policy, allowing governments to regulate the economy through changes in tax rates and policies.

Overall, taxation is a complex and dynamic system that serves as the lifeblood of a nation's financial health and supports its socioeconomic development. It requires careful consideration and balancing of various economic, social, and political factors to achieve optimal outcomes for both governments and citizens.

Historical Development of Taxation

The historical development of taxation dates back thousands of years and has evolved significantly over time. Here is an overview of the key milestones in the history of taxation:

1. Ancient Civilizations: Taxation can be traced back to ancient civilizations such as Mesopotamia, Egypt, and ancient Greece, where rulers imposed taxes on agricultural production, trade, and other economic activities. These taxes were primarily used to fund the military and public infrastructure.

2. Roman Empire: The Roman Empire had a well-developed tax system, including taxes on property, sales, and inheritance. Taxes were collected to finance the vast empire and its military campaigns.

3. Medieval Period: During the medieval period, feudal lords and monarchs collected taxes from their subjects to maintain their authority and finance wars. The concept of "feudal dues" and "tithe" emerged, where peasants were required to give a portion of their agricultural produce to the ruling classes and the church.

4. Early Modern Era: The emergence of nation-states in the early modern era saw the development of more organized and centralized tax systems. In Europe, taxes on imports and exports became prevalent, contributing to the growth of mercantilism and the expansion of colonial empires.

5. American Revolution: Taxation played a significant role in the American Revolution against British rule. The

famous slogan "No taxation without representation" reflected the colonists' demand for a say in how they were taxed.

6. 19th Century: The 19th century witnessed the rise of income taxation in various countries. The introduction of income taxes provided governments with a stable source of revenue to finance growing social and industrial needs.

7. World Wars: The two World Wars saw a significant increase in taxation to fund the war efforts. Income tax rates were raised, and new forms of taxes, such as excess profits tax, were introduced.

8. Modern Taxation: In the post-World War II era, many countries developed complex tax systems, including income tax, corporate tax, sales tax, and property tax. Governments continue to use taxation as a tool for economic management and social welfare programs.

9. Globalization: With the rise of globalization, tax policies have become increasingly interconnected. Countries negotiate tax treaties and agreements to prevent double taxation and promote cross-border trade and investment.

10. Digital Economy: The digital economy has posed challenges for taxation, as traditional tax systems struggle to capture revenue from online transactions and global tech giants. Many countries are now exploring ways to tax digital services and products effectively.

Throughout history, taxation has been shaped by economic, political, and social factors, reflecting the changing needs and priorities of societies. Today, taxation remains a critical instrument for governments to fund public services, promote economic growth, and achieve various policy objectives.

Taxation and Social Policy

Taxation and social policy are closely interconnected, as the way taxes are designed and implemented can have significant implications for social and economic outcomes. Taxation is not only a means for governments to raise revenue but also a tool for achieving social objectives and redistributing wealth. Here are some key aspects of the relationship between taxation and social policy:

1. Income Redistribution: Progressive taxation, where higher-income individuals pay a larger proportion of their income in taxes, is often used as a mechanism for income redistribution. By taxing the wealthy more than the poor, governments can transfer resources from higher-income groups to lower-income groups, reducing income inequality and promoting social equity.

2. Social Welfare Programs: Tax revenues are often used to fund social welfare programs, such as healthcare, education, housing assistance, and unemployment benefits. These programs aim to provide a safety net for vulnerable populations and improve overall social well-being.

3. Tax Credits and Deductions: Tax credits and deductions can be targeted to support specific social objectives. For example, tax credits for low-income families, child tax credits, and education-related deductions can help alleviate financial burdens and support social mobility.

4. Behavioral Incentives: Taxation can be used to influence individual behavior and promote socially desirable

outcomes. For instance, governments may use taxes on harmful activities like tobacco and alcohol to discourage consumption and improve public health.

5. Environmental Policies: Taxation can also be employed to address environmental challenges. Carbon taxes and other environmental levies aim to reduce carbon emissions and incentivize businesses and individuals to adopt more eco-friendly practices.

6. Tax Expenditures: Some tax policies, such as tax breaks and incentives for certain industries or activities, can be viewed as social policies. These tax expenditures are designed to encourage specific behaviors or stimulate economic growth in targeted sectors.

7. Fiscal Policy and Economic Stability: Taxation is a crucial component of fiscal policy, which governments use to stabilize the economy during economic downturns or periods of inflation. Tax changes can impact consumer spending, business investment, and overall economic activity.

8. Tax Compliance and Enforcement: Social policy objectives can also influence tax compliance and enforcement strategies. Governments may prioritize initiatives to combat tax evasion and promote tax fairness to ensure that everyone contributes their fair share to support social programs.

Overall, the design and implementation of taxation play a significant role in shaping social policy and determining the level of social support and services available to citizens. Effective taxation policies can contribute to a more equitable and inclusive society by redistributing resources, supporting vulnerable populations, and achieving broader social objectives.

Foundations of Tax Law

Foundations of tax law refer to the fundamental principles and concepts that form the basis of taxation systems in various countries. These foundations provide the framework for levying, collecting, and regulating taxes. Some of the key foundations of tax law include:

1. Legal Authority: Taxation is based on the principle of legal authority, meaning that governments have the legal power to impose and collect taxes from individuals and businesses. This authority is typically derived from legislation, such as tax codes and statutes, passed by the legislature.

2. Taxable Event: Taxation is triggered by a taxable event, which is the occurrence that gives rise to the tax liability. The taxable event varies depending on the type of tax, such as income earned (income tax), goods purchased (sales tax), or property owned (property tax).

3. Taxable Base: The taxable base is the value or amount on which the tax is calculated. For example, in income tax, the taxable base is the individual's or business's taxable income, while in sales tax, it is the purchase price of goods and services.

4. Tax Rates: Tax rates are the percentages or fixed amounts applied to the taxable base to determine the actual amount of tax owed. Tax rates can be progressive, regressive, or proportional, depending on the tax system.

5. Tax Liability and Payment: Tax liability refers to the amount of tax an individual or business owes to the

government. Taxpayers are required to pay their taxes based on specific deadlines and payment methods outlined in tax laws.

6. Taxation Authorities: Taxation authorities, such as tax agencies or revenue services, are responsible for administering and enforcing tax laws. They have the authority to conduct audits, collect taxes, and address any tax-related disputes or issues.

7. Taxation Principles: Various principles guide the development of tax laws, including equity, efficiency, simplicity, and certainty. These principles aim to create a fair and effective tax system that promotes economic growth and minimizes compliance costs.

8. Tax Planning and Avoidance: Tax planning involves legally arranging financial affairs to minimize tax liability. While tax planning is acceptable, tax avoidance, which involves using loopholes or artificial transactions to reduce taxes beyond the intent of the law, may be subject to anti-avoidance provisions.

9. Tax Treaties: Tax treaties are agreements between countries to prevent double taxation and resolve tax issues related to international transactions. These treaties help facilitate cross-border trade and investment.

10. Tax Policy: Tax policy refers to the government's overall approach to taxation, including the goals, objectives, and priorities of the tax system. Tax policy decisions can impact economic growth, income distribution, and social welfare.

Understanding the foundations of tax law is essential for taxpayers, tax professionals, and policymakers to navigate the complexities of taxation and ensure compliance with the law. It provides the groundwork for creating an effective and fair tax system that meets the needs of society and supports government revenue requirements.

Constitutional Basis for Taxation

The constitutional basis for taxation refers to the legal authority and framework provided by a country's constitution for levying and collecting taxes. In most democratic nations, including the United States, taxation is authorized and regulated by the country's constitution. The constitutional provisions related to taxation play a crucial role in defining the scope, limits, and principles of the tax system.

In the United States, the constitutional basis for taxation is primarily derived from the following provisions:

1. Taxing Power: Article I, Section 8 of the United States Constitution grants Congress the power to lay and collect taxes, duties, imposts, and excises. This provision is known as the "Taxing and Spending Clause" or "Tax Clause." It empowers Congress to raise revenue for the federal government through various forms of taxation.

2. Direct Taxes and Apportionment: The Constitution distinguishes between direct taxes and indirect taxes. Direct taxes, such as property taxes or income taxes, must be apportioned among the states based on their respective populations. This requirement is outlined in Article I, Section 2, and Article I, Section 9.

3. Uniformity of Duties, Imposts, and Excises: Article I, Section 8 also specifies that all duties, imposts, and excises must be uniform throughout the United States. This means that Congress cannot impose different tax rates or rules on different states or regions.

4. Sixteenth Amendment: The Sixteenth Amendment to

the United States Constitution, ratified in 1913, granted Congress the power to levy income taxes without the need for apportionment among the states. This amendment expanded the scope of federal income taxation.

Apart from the federal level, state constitutions also provide the constitutional basis for taxation at the state level. Each state's constitution outlines the powers and limitations of its own taxing authority, which may vary from state to state.

The constitutional basis for taxation ensures that the government's power to tax is exercised in a lawful and accountable manner. It establishes the framework for the distribution of tax revenue, the types of taxes that can be levied, and the rules governing tax administration. By providing clear guidelines, the constitutional provisions on taxation protect taxpayers' rights and promote transparency and fairness in the tax system.

Taxation Authorities and Agencies

Taxation authorities and agencies are government bodies responsible for administering and enforcing tax laws and regulations. These agencies play a crucial role in collecting taxes, ensuring compliance, and providing taxpayer assistance. The specific names and structures of these agencies may vary from country to country, but their primary functions and objectives remain similar. Some of the key taxation authorities and agencies around the world include:

1. Internal Revenue Service (IRS) - United States: The IRS is the federal agency responsible for administering and enforcing the tax laws in the United States. It collects federal income taxes and oversees various other tax-related matters.

2. Her Majesty's Revenue and Customs (HMRC) - United Kingdom: HMRC is the UK's tax authority responsible for collecting taxes, enforcing tax laws, and providing taxpayer services.

3. Canada Revenue Agency (CRA) - Canada: The CRA is the federal agency in Canada responsible for administering tax laws and collecting federal taxes, including income taxes and goods and services taxes (GST).

4. Australian Taxation Office (ATO) - Australia: The ATO is the principal tax authority in Australia, responsible for administering the tax system and collecting various taxes, including income tax, goods and services tax (GST), and others.

5. Bundeszentralamt für Steuern (BZSt) - Germany: BZSt is the central tax office in Germany responsible for

administering various taxes, including income tax, corporate tax, and value-added tax (VAT).

6. Tax and Customs Administration (Belastingdienst) - Netherlands: The Tax and Customs Administration is the Dutch tax authority responsible for collecting taxes and customs duties.

7. Servicio de Impuestos Internos (SII) - Chile: The SII is the tax authority in Chile responsible for collecting taxes, including income tax and value-added tax (VAT).

8. State Revenue Offices - Various Countries: Many countries have state-level revenue offices that handle tax administration and collections at the state or provincial level.

These taxation authorities and agencies have the mandate to assess, collect, and audit taxes, provide guidance to taxpayers, and enforce tax compliance. They also work to combat tax evasion and fraud and conduct outreach programs to educate taxpayers about their tax obligations and rights. Taxation agencies are an essential part of the government's revenue collection efforts and contribute to the functioning of public services and infrastructure.

Tax Policy and Legislative Process

Tax policy refers to the government's approach to levying and collecting taxes. It involves decisions about the types of taxes to impose, the rates at which they are levied, and the overall objectives of the tax system. The tax policy is an essential aspect of fiscal policy and plays a significant role in shaping a country's economic and social landscape.

The legislative process is the mechanism through which tax policies are formulated and enacted into law. It involves various steps, including proposal, debate, amendment, and approval, before the tax laws are implemented. The legislative process typically involves the following stages:

1. Proposal: Tax policies are proposed by government officials, policymakers, or tax experts. These proposals may be part of the annual budget or can be introduced as standalone tax legislation.
2. Introduction: The proposed tax legislation is introduced in the legislature, such as the parliament or congress, as a bill.
3. Committee Review: The bill is referred to a committee that specializes in tax matters. The committee reviews the proposed legislation and may hold hearings to gather input from stakeholders and experts.
4. Debate: The bill is debated by members of the legislature, who discuss its merits and potential impact. Amendments may be proposed during the debate.
5. Voting: After the debate, the bill is put to a vote. If it is approved by a majority, it moves to the next stage.
6. Approval: The bill is sent to the executive branch for

      approval by the head of state or government. Once approved, it becomes law.

7. Implementation: The tax law is implemented by the tax authorities, who are responsible for collecting taxes and enforcing compliance.

Throughout the legislative process, various factors influence the development of tax policies, including economic conditions, social needs, political considerations, and public opinion. Tax policy decisions have far-reaching implications on the distribution of wealth, economic growth, investment, and social welfare. It is essential for governments to carefully consider these factors and strike a balance between revenue needs and the impact of taxes on individuals, businesses, and the overall economy.

In many countries, tax policy is an ongoing and dynamic process, with changes and adjustments made as needed to adapt to changing economic and social conditions. Tax policy decisions are often subject to public scrutiny and debate, and policymakers must consider the diverse perspectives and interests of various stakeholders to develop effective and fair tax policies.

Taxpayer Rights and Responsibilities

Taxpayer rights and responsibilities are essential components of any tax system. They ensure that taxpayers are treated fairly and transparently while fulfilling their obligations to contribute to the public revenue. Here is an overview of taxpayer rights and responsibilities:

Taxpayer Rights:

1. Right to Information: Taxpayers have the right to be informed about their tax obligations, including the types of taxes they are required to pay, the applicable rates, and any changes in tax laws.
2. Right to Privacy: Taxpayers have the right to privacy concerning their financial and tax-related information. Tax authorities must keep taxpayer information confidential and use it only for legitimate tax purposes.
3. Right to Representation: Taxpayers have the right to be represented by a tax professional or advocate during tax audits, disputes, and other interactions with tax authorities.
4. Right to Appeal: Taxpayers have the right to challenge tax assessments and decisions through an appeals process. They can seek a review of their tax liabilities and dispute any errors or discrepancies.
5. Right to Fair Treatment: Taxpayers have the right to be treated fairly and impartially by tax authorities. They should not be subject to discrimination or arbitrary actions.
6. Right to Timely Responses: Taxpayers have the right to receive timely responses from tax authorities regarding

their tax inquiries, requests for information, and applications for tax refunds.

7. Right to Correctness: Taxpayers have the right to expect that their tax assessments are based on accurate and complete information.

Taxpayer Responsibilities:

1. Filing Tax Returns: Taxpayers are responsible for filing their tax returns accurately and on time. This includes reporting all income and claiming eligible deductions and credits.

2. Paying Taxes: Taxpayers are responsible for paying the correct amount of taxes owed on time. Failure to do so may result in penalties and interest.

3. Maintaining Records: Taxpayers are responsible for maintaining adequate records and documents to support the information reported on their tax returns.

4. Reporting Changes: Taxpayers are responsible for informing tax authorities of any changes in their personal or financial circumstances that may affect their tax liabilities.

5. Cooperation with Tax Audits: Taxpayers are required to cooperate with tax authorities during tax audits and provide requested information and documents.

6. Reporting Offshore Assets: Taxpayers with offshore financial assets may have additional reporting requirements, such as the Foreign Account Tax Compliance Act (FATCA) in the United States.

7. Complying with Tax Laws: Taxpayers are responsible for understanding and complying with all applicable tax laws and regulations.

Both taxpayers and tax authorities play crucial roles in ensuring the functioning and effectiveness of the tax system. By upholding taxpayer rights and fulfilling their responsibilities, taxpayers contribute to the fair and efficient administration of taxes, which, in turn, supports government revenue and public services.

Individual Income Taxation

Individual income taxation is the system by which governments impose taxes on the income earned by individuals. It is a significant source of revenue for governments and is used to fund public services and programs. Here is an overview of individual income taxation:

1. Taxable Income: Individual income tax is typically based on taxable income, which includes wages, salaries, tips, self-employment income, interest, dividends, and other sources of income. Certain deductions and credits may reduce the amount of taxable income.

2. Tax Rates: Individual income tax rates are progressive, meaning that higher levels of income are subject to higher tax rates. The tax rates are set by the government and can vary depending on the taxpayer's filing status (e.g., single, married filing jointly, head of household) and level of income.

3. Filing Status: Taxpayers must choose a filing status that determines their tax rates and eligibility for certain deductions and credits. Common filing statuses include single, married filing jointly, married filing separately, and head of household.

4. Deductions and Credits: Taxpayers may claim deductions to reduce their taxable income. Common deductions include those for mortgage interest, student loan interest, and charitable contributions. Additionally, tax credits can directly reduce the amount of tax owed.

5. Withholding and Estimated Taxes: Many taxpayers have taxes withheld from their paychecks by their employers throughout the year. Others, such as self-employed individuals, must make estimated tax payments on a quarterly basis.

6. Tax Returns: Taxpayers must file income tax returns each year, typically by April 15th (or the next business day if April 15th falls on a weekend or holiday). The tax return calculates the final tax liability, and any overpayment of taxes may result in a tax refund.

7. Tax Planning: Taxpayers can engage in tax planning to legally minimize their tax liability. This may involve making strategic decisions about deductions, credits, and investment choices.

8. Tax Compliance: Taxpayers are responsible for complying with all applicable tax laws and regulations. Failure to do so may result in penalties and interest.

Individual income taxation can be complex, and tax laws may vary by jurisdiction. Taxpayers often seek the assistance of tax professionals or use tax software to navigate the complexities of the tax code and ensure accurate and timely filing. Understanding individual income taxation is essential for individuals to fulfill their tax obligations and make informed financial decisions.

Income Tax Basics and Filing Requirements

Income tax is a tax imposed by governments on the income earned by individuals and businesses. It is a key source of revenue for governments and is used to fund various public services and programs.

Income tax basics include the following key points:

1. Taxable Income: Taxable income is the amount of income that is subject to tax after deducting allowable deductions and exemptions. It includes wages, salaries, tips, business income, rental income, interest, dividends, and other sources of income.

2. Tax Rates: Income tax rates are usually progressive, meaning that higher levels of income are subject to higher tax rates. The tax rates are set by the government and can vary depending on the taxpayer's filing status and level of income.

3. Filing Status: Taxpayers must choose a filing status when filing their tax returns. Common filing statuses include single, married filing jointly, married filing separately, and head of household. The filing status determines the tax rates and standard deduction available to the taxpayer.

4. Tax Deductions and Credits: Taxpayers can reduce their taxable income through deductions and tax credits. Deductions are expenses that can be subtracted from taxable income, such as mortgage interest, student loan

interest, and medical expenses. Tax credits directly reduce the amount of tax owed, such as the child tax credit or earned income tax credit.

5. Tax Forms and Filing: Taxpayers must use the appropriate tax forms to report their income and calculate their tax liability. Commonly used forms include Form 1040 for individuals and Form 1120 for businesses. Taxpayers must file their tax returns by the due date, which is typically April 15th (or the next business day if April 15th falls on a weekend or holiday).

6. Withholding and Estimated Taxes: Many employees have income tax withheld from their paychecks by their employers throughout the year. Self-employed individuals and others who do not have taxes withheld must make estimated tax payments on a quarterly basis.

7. Refunds and Payments: After filing their tax returns, taxpayers may receive a tax refund if they overpaid their taxes throughout the year. If taxes owed exceed the amount withheld or paid in estimated taxes, the taxpayer must make a payment to cover the remaining tax liability.

Filing requirements vary based on income levels, filing status, and other factors. Generally, individuals whose income exceeds a certain threshold are required to file a tax return. However, some low-income individuals may be exempt from filing if their income is below a specified threshold.

It's essential for taxpayers to understand income tax basics and their filing requirements to ensure compliance with tax laws and avoid penalties for non-compliance. Many taxpayers seek assistance from tax professionals or use tax software to help them accurately calculate their tax liability and file their tax returns correctly.

Deductions, Exemptions, and Credits

Deductions, exemptions, and credits are important components of the tax code that help taxpayers reduce their taxable income and lower their overall tax liability. Each of these elements serves a different purpose and can have a significant impact on a taxpayer's tax bill.

1. Deductions: Deductions are expenses that taxpayers are allowed to subtract from their taxable income, thereby reducing the amount of income that is subject to tax. There are two types of deductions: standard deductions and itemized deductions.

   - Standard Deduction: The standard deduction is a fixed amount that taxpayers can subtract from their taxable income without having to itemize their deductions. The standard deduction amount varies depending on the taxpayer's filing status and is set by the government each year.

   - Itemized Deductions: Taxpayers who have deductible expenses that exceed the standard deduction amount may choose to itemize their deductions instead. Itemized deductions can include expenses such as mortgage interest, state and local taxes, medical expenses, charitable contributions, and certain job-related expenses.

2. Exemptions: Exemptions are a predetermined amount that taxpayers can subtract from their taxable income for themselves, their spouse, and each eligible dependent. Before the passage of the Tax Cuts and Jobs Act in 2017, taxpayers could claim a personal exemption

for themselves and each dependent. However, under the new tax law, personal exemptions have been temporarily suspended, but the child tax credit and other credits have been expanded to offset this change.

3. Tax Credits: Tax credits are dollar-for-dollar reductions in a taxpayer's tax liability. Unlike deductions and exemptions, which reduce taxable income, tax credits directly reduce the amount of tax owed. There are two types of tax credits: refundable and non-refundable.

- Refundable Credits: Refundable credits can result in a tax refund even if the credit amount exceeds the taxpayer's total tax liability. For example, if a taxpayer owes $1,000 in taxes but is eligible for a $1,500 refundable credit, they will receive a $500 refund.

- Non-Refundable Credits: Non-refundable credits can reduce a taxpayer's tax liability to zero, but they cannot result in a tax refund. If a taxpayer's tax liability is already reduced to zero, any excess non-refundable credit amount is forfeited.

Common tax credits include the child tax credit, earned income tax credit, education credits, and energy-saving credits.

It's essential for taxpayers to understand the deductions, exemptions, and credits available to them to take full advantage of tax-saving opportunities. The choice between taking the standard deduction or itemizing deductions and understanding eligibility for various credits can significantly impact a taxpayer's tax liability. Taxpayers can use tax software or consult with tax professionals to ensure they optimize their tax-saving opportunities while remaining compliant with tax laws.

Tax Planning for Individuals

Tax planning for individuals is the process of making strategic financial decisions throughout the year to minimize tax liability and maximize after-tax income. Effective tax planning involves understanding the tax code, identifying potential deductions and credits, and structuring financial transactions in a tax-efficient manner. Here are some key strategies for tax planning for individuals:

1. Understand Tax Brackets: Know the tax brackets that apply to your income level and adjust your income to stay within a lower tax bracket whenever possible.

2. Contribute to Retirement Accounts: Contributions to tax-advantaged retirement accounts, such as 401(k)s and IRAs, can reduce taxable income and defer taxes on investment earnings.

3. Utilize Tax Deductions: Take advantage of available tax deductions, such as mortgage interest, medical expenses, state and local taxes, and charitable contributions. Consider itemizing deductions if they exceed the standard deduction.

4. Consider Tax Credits: Research and claim applicable tax credits, such as the child tax credit, earned income tax credit, education credits, and energy-saving credits, to directly reduce tax liability.

5. Timing of Income and Expenses: Time the receipt of income and payment of expenses to optimize tax benefits. For example, defer income to the following year or accelerate deductible expenses into the current year.

6. Capital Gains and Losses: Consider the tax implications of capital gains and losses on investments. Selling investments with capital losses can offset gains and reduce tax liability.
7. Health Savings Accounts (HSAs): Contribute to an HSA if eligible, as it allows for tax-free contributions and withdrawals for qualified medical expenses.
8. Charitable Giving: Charitable contributions can be tax-deductible, so consider donating to qualified charities to reduce taxable income.
9. Tax-Efficient Investments: Choose investments that generate tax-efficient income, such as municipal bonds, which are tax-free at the federal level.
10. Filing Status: Select the most advantageous filing status, such as married filing jointly or head of household, to optimize tax benefits.
11. Consider Tax Implications of Life Events: Be aware of the tax consequences of major life events, such as marriage, divorce, home purchase, or retirement.
12. Estate Planning: Plan for the transfer of assets to heirs efficiently, considering estate tax implications and utilizing tools like trusts and gifting.

It is crucial to start tax planning early in the year and continuously review financial decisions throughout the year to ensure tax efficiency. Taxpayers can benefit from seeking advice from tax professionals or using tax software to navigate the complexities of the tax code and implement effective tax planning strategies tailored to their individual circumstances.

Taxation of Investment Income

Taxation of investment income refers to the taxation of earnings and gains generated from various types of investments. The taxation of investment income can vary depending on the type of investment, the holding period, and the investor's overall tax situation. Here are some common types of investment income and their tax treatment:

1. Dividends: Dividends received from stocks and mutual funds are generally taxed at different rates depending on whether they are qualified or non-qualified dividends. Qualified dividends are taxed at the capital gains tax rate, which is typically lower than the ordinary income tax rate. Non-qualified dividends are taxed at the individual's ordinary income tax rate.

2. Capital Gains: Capital gains result from the sale of investments such as stocks, bonds, real estate, and other assets. Short-term capital gains (investments held for one year or less) are typically taxed at the individual's ordinary income tax rate, while long-term capital gains (investments held for more than one year) are generally taxed at a lower rate.

3. Interest Income: Interest earned from investments such as bonds, savings accounts, and certificates of deposit (CDs) is generally taxed as ordinary income at the individual's applicable tax rate.

4. Rental Income: Rental income generated from real estate properties is generally considered ordinary income and is taxed at the individual's applicable tax rate. However, there are certain deductions and credits

available to offset rental income.

5. Passive Income: Passive income from limited partnerships, real estate investments, and other passive activities may be subject to the passive activity loss rules, which limit the ability to deduct losses against other sources of income.

6. Retirement Accounts: Income earned within tax-advantaged retirement accounts, such as 401(k)s and IRAs, is tax-deferred until withdrawn. Withdrawals from traditional retirement accounts are generally taxed as ordinary income, while withdrawals from Roth accounts are typically tax-free.

7. Municipal Bonds: Interest earned from municipal bonds is generally exempt from federal income tax and may also be exempt from state and local taxes if the investor resides in the issuing municipality.

8. Foreign Investment Income: Foreign investment income may be subject to additional tax reporting requirements and may be taxed at different rates depending on international tax treaties and laws.

It's essential for investors to understand the tax implications of their investment decisions and to plan accordingly to minimize tax liability. Tax-efficient investing, such as holding investments in tax-advantaged accounts or using tax-loss harvesting strategies, can help optimize after-tax returns. Investors should consult with a tax professional or financial advisor to develop a tax-efficient investment strategy tailored to their specific financial goals and circumstances.

Retirement Accounts and Taxation

Retirement accounts play a crucial role in helping individuals save for their retirement while also providing tax benefits. There are several types of retirement accounts, each with its own tax treatment. Here are some common retirement accounts and their taxation:

1. Traditional Individual Retirement Account (IRA): Contributions to a traditional IRA are made with pre-tax dollars, meaning they are tax-deductible in the year they are made. The earnings within the account grow tax-deferred, and withdrawals in retirement are treated as ordinary income and subject to income tax at the individual's applicable tax rate.

2. Roth Individual Retirement Account (Roth IRA): Contributions to a Roth IRA are made with after-tax dollars, so they are not tax-deductible in the year they are made. However, the earnings within the account grow tax-free, and qualified withdrawals in retirement are tax-free. Additionally, Roth IRAs do not have required minimum distributions (RMDs) during the account owner's lifetime.

3. Employer-Sponsored Retirement Plans (e.g., 401(k), 403(b)): Contributions to employer-sponsored retirement plans are typically made with pre-tax dollars, reducing the individual's taxable income in the year of contribution. Similar to traditional IRAs, the earnings in these plans grow tax-deferred, and withdrawals in retirement are treated as ordinary income.

4. Roth 401(k) and Roth 403(b): Some employer-

sponsored retirement plans also offer a Roth option, allowing employees to make after-tax contributions. The earnings in these plans grow tax-free, and qualified withdrawals in retirement are tax-free.

5. Simplified Employee Pension (SEP) IRA and Savings Incentive Match Plan for Employees (SIMPLE) IRA: These retirement plans are designed for self-employed individuals and small business owners. Contributions are tax-deductible for the employer and are made with pre-tax dollars for employees. Withdrawals in retirement are treated as ordinary income.

6. Social Security Benefits: Social Security benefits may be subject to income tax, depending on the individual's total income and filing status. Up to 85% of Social Security benefits can be included in taxable income for certain high-income retirees.

It's important to note that early withdrawals from retirement accounts before the age of 59½ may be subject to a 10% early withdrawal penalty in addition to income tax (with some exceptions, such as for certain hardship distributions or qualifying distributions from Roth IRAs).

Taxation of retirement accounts can be complex, and the rules may change over time. It is advisable for individuals to consult with a tax professional or financial advisor to understand the specific tax implications of their retirement savings and to develop a retirement strategy that aligns with their financial goals and tax situation.

Taxation of Business Income for Sole Proprietors

As a sole proprietor, the taxation of business income is relatively straightforward, as there is no legal distinction between the business and the individual. Here are the key points to understand about the taxation of business income for sole proprietors:

1. Pass-through Entity: A sole proprietorship is considered a pass-through entity for tax purposes. This means that the business income is not taxed at the business level. Instead, the business income "passes through" to the individual owner's personal tax return.

2. Reporting Income and Expenses: The owner of a sole proprietorship reports business income and expenses on Schedule C (Form 1040) when filing their personal tax return. The net income or loss from the business is then included in the owner's total taxable income.

3. Self-Employment Tax: In addition to regular income tax, sole proprietors are also subject to self-employment tax, which covers both the employer and employee portions of Social Security and Medicare taxes. The self-employment tax is calculated based on the net income from the business.

4. Estimated Tax Payments: Sole proprietors are generally required to make estimated tax payments throughout the year if they expect to owe $1,000 or more in tax after subtracting withholding and credits. Estimated tax payments help sole proprietors avoid underpayment penalties.

5. Deductions: Sole proprietors can deduct ordinary and necessary business expenses to reduce their taxable income. Common deductions include business supplies, equipment, travel expenses, advertising, and home office expenses if the owner uses a portion of their home for business purposes.
6. Retirement Savings: Sole proprietors can contribute to tax-advantaged retirement plans, such as a Simplified Employee Pension (SEP) IRA or a Solo 401(k), to save for retirement while potentially reducing taxable income.
7. Tax Filing Deadline: Sole proprietors must file their personal tax returns, including Schedule C, by the individual income tax filing deadline, which is usually April 15th.

It is important for sole proprietors to maintain accurate and organized records of their business income and expenses to ensure proper reporting and to take advantage of all available deductions. Consulting with a tax professional or accountant can be beneficial to ensure compliance with tax laws and to maximize tax-saving opportunities for sole proprietors.

Corporate Taxation

Corporate taxation is the system of taxing income earned by corporations or business entities. Here are the key aspects of corporate taxation:

1. Corporate Tax Rate: Corporations are subject to income tax on their profits, known as corporate tax. The tax rate varies depending on the country and the level of income earned by the corporation.
2. Legal Entity: Corporations are considered separate legal entities from their owners. As a result, they are taxed as distinct entities, and the profits and losses of the corporation are not directly attributed to the shareholders.
3. Double Taxation: Corporate taxation is often associated with double taxation, as corporations pay income tax on their profits, and shareholders may also pay tax on dividends they receive from the corporation. However, some jurisdictions have introduced measures to mitigate double taxation.
4. Filing Requirements: Corporations are required to file tax returns with the tax authorities, reporting their income, deductions, and other financial information. The tax return provides the basis for calculating the corporation's tax liability.
5. Deductions and Credits: Like individuals, corporations can claim deductions and tax credits to reduce their taxable income. Common deductions for corporations include business expenses, depreciation of assets, and interest on business loans.

6. Tax Treatments: Different types of corporations, such as C corporations and S corporations in the United States, have different tax treatments. C corporations are subject to corporate tax at the entity level, while S corporations are pass-through entities, and their income is taxed at the individual shareholder level.

7. International Taxation: Multinational corporations may face complex tax issues due to their operations in multiple countries. International taxation involves considerations of transfer pricing, foreign tax credits, and tax treaties.

8. Estimated Tax Payments: Corporations may be required to make estimated tax payments throughout the year if they expect to owe a certain amount of tax. This helps corporations avoid underpayment penalties.

9. Tax Planning: Corporations often engage in tax planning to minimize their tax liability legally. This may involve timing income and expenses, using tax-efficient investment strategies, and taking advantage of tax credits and incentives.

10. Compliance and Reporting: Corporate taxation requires adherence to complex tax laws and regulations. Corporations must maintain accurate financial records and comply with reporting requirements to ensure proper tax filings.

It is essential for corporations to stay up-to-date with tax laws and work with tax professionals or accountants to navigate the complexities of corporate taxation and optimize their tax position while remaining compliant with tax regulations.

Corporate Tax Basics and Filing Requirements

Corporate tax basics and filing requirements involve the taxation of income earned by corporations or business entities. Here are the key points:

1. Corporate Tax Rate: The corporate tax rate is the percentage at which a corporation's taxable income is taxed. The rate varies by country and may differ based on the level of income earned by the corporation.

2. Legal Entity: Corporations are separate legal entities from their owners, and they are taxed as distinct entities. The profits and losses of the corporation are not directly attributed to the shareholders.

3. Filing Tax Returns: Corporations are required to file annual tax returns with the tax authorities. The tax return provides information about the corporation's income, deductions, credits, and other financial data used to calculate the tax liability.

4. Taxable Income: To calculate the corporate tax liability, taxable income is determined by subtracting allowable deductions and exemptions from the corporation's total income.

5. Deductions and Credits: Corporations can claim deductions and tax credits to reduce their taxable income. Common deductions include business expenses, depreciation of assets, and interest on business loans.

6. Estimated Tax Payments: Corporations may be required

to make estimated tax payments throughout the year if they expect to owe a certain amount of tax. Estimated tax payments help corporations avoid underpayment penalties.

7. Filing Deadlines: The deadline for filing corporate tax returns varies by jurisdiction. In the United States, the deadline is generally March 15 for calendar-year corporations and the 15th day of the third month after the end of the fiscal year for fiscal-year corporations.

8. E-filing: Many jurisdictions allow corporations to e-file their tax returns, which offers a more convenient and faster method of submitting tax information to the tax authorities.

9. Compliance and Reporting: Corporate taxation requires adherence to complex tax laws and regulations. Corporations must maintain accurate financial records and comply with reporting requirements to ensure proper tax filings.

10. Tax Planning: Corporations may engage in tax planning to minimize their tax liability legally. Tax planning involves strategic decisions related to timing income and expenses, using tax-efficient investment strategies, and taking advantage of tax credits and incentives.

It is essential for corporations to understand their corporate tax obligations and work with tax professionals or accountants to ensure compliance with tax laws and optimize their tax position. Failure to comply with tax regulations can result in penalties and legal consequences. Therefore, corporations should prioritize accurate and timely tax reporting to stay in good standing with tax authorities.

Tax Treatment of Business Expenses and Deductions

The tax treatment of business expenses and deductions is an essential aspect of corporate taxation. Corporations can deduct various expenses from their taxable income to reduce their tax liability. Here are some common business expenses and deductions:

1. Ordinary and Necessary Expenses: Businesses can deduct expenses that are both ordinary and necessary for their trade or business. Ordinary expenses are those commonly incurred in the industry, while necessary expenses are essential for the business's operations.
2. Salaries and Wages: The salaries and wages paid to employees are deductible business expenses. This includes wages, salaries, bonuses, commissions, and benefits.
3. Rent and Lease Payments: Rent paid for business premises, equipment, or vehicles can be deducted as a business expense.
4. Supplies and Materials: The cost of supplies and materials used in the business, such as office supplies, raw materials, and inventory, are deductible.
5. Business Travel and Meals: Business-related travel expenses, such as airfare, hotel accommodations, and meals, may be deducted. However, there are specific rules and limitations for deducting meal expenses.
6. Advertising and Marketing: The costs associated with advertising and marketing efforts, including online

advertising, print materials, and promotional events, are deductible.

7. Insurance Premiums: Premiums paid for business insurance, such as liability insurance and property insurance, can be deducted.

8. Depreciation: Businesses can deduct the cost of tangible assets (e.g., machinery, equipment, buildings) over their useful life through depreciation deductions.

9. Interest Expense: Interest on business loans, credit lines, and other financing arrangements is generally deductible.

10. Bad Debts: If a business is unable to collect payment for goods or services provided to customers, it may be able to deduct the amount as a bad debt expense.

11. Research and Development (R&D) Expenses: Certain R&D expenses may be deductible or eligible for tax credits, depending on the tax laws of the jurisdiction.

It is essential for businesses to maintain accurate records of their expenses and ensure that they meet the criteria for deductibility. Some expenses may have specific limitations or exclusions, and tax laws can vary by jurisdiction. Working with tax professionals or accountants can help businesses identify and properly deduct eligible business expenses, ensuring compliance with tax regulations while maximizing tax savings.

Taxation of Corporate Distributions and Dividends

The taxation of corporate distributions and dividends is an important aspect of corporate taxation. Corporate distributions refer to the distribution of profits or assets from a corporation to its shareholders. Dividends, which are a common form of corporate distribution, are typically paid to shareholders in proportion to their ownership of the company's stock.

Here are the key points regarding the taxation of corporate distributions and dividends:

1. Tax Treatment: Dividends received by individual shareholders are generally taxable as ordinary income. However, certain dividends may qualify for preferential tax rates, such as qualified dividends, which are taxed at lower capital gains tax rates.

2. Qualified Dividends: To be considered qualified dividends, the dividends must meet specific criteria set forth by tax laws. Generally, the shareholder must hold the stock for a minimum period, and the dividends must be paid by a U.S. corporation or a qualifying foreign corporation.

3. Corporate Tax Deduction: Corporations may deduct dividends paid to shareholders as business expenses, reducing their taxable income.

4. Double Taxation: Corporate distributions, including dividends, are subject to double taxation. The corporation pays corporate income tax on its profits,

and then individual shareholders pay taxes on the dividends they receive from those after-tax profits.

5. Dividend Tax Withholding: In some jurisdictions, companies are required to withhold taxes on dividends paid to foreign shareholders. The withholding rates may vary based on tax treaties and local tax laws.

6. Stock Buybacks: Corporations may also repurchase their own stock from shareholders, which can have tax implications for both the corporation and the shareholders.

7. Retained Earnings: Corporations can also choose to retain earnings and reinvest them in the business rather than distributing them as dividends. This can result in tax deferral for shareholders until they eventually sell their shares.

It is important for corporations and shareholders to understand the tax implications of corporate distributions and dividends to effectively manage their tax planning and compliance. Tax laws regarding corporate distributions and dividends can be complex and vary by jurisdiction, so seeking professional tax advice is advisable for both corporations and individual shareholders.

International Tax Planning for Corporations

International tax planning for corporations involves strategies to minimize tax liabilities and optimize financial efficiency across different countries and jurisdictions where a corporation operates. The goal is to take advantage of favorable tax regimes, avoid unnecessary tax burdens, and comply with tax laws in each country while achieving the best possible overall tax outcome for the corporation.

Here are some key considerations and strategies involved in international tax planning for corporations:

1. Tax Residency and Permanent Establishment: Determining the tax residency of the corporation and whether it has a permanent establishment in a foreign country is crucial as it affects the corporation's tax obligations in that country.
2. Transfer Pricing: Managing transfer pricing is important for corporations with related entities operating in different countries. Transfer pricing rules ensure that transactions between related parties are conducted at arm's length, preventing tax base erosion.
3. Tax Treaties: Utilizing tax treaties between countries can help corporations reduce or eliminate double taxation on income earned in multiple jurisdictions.
4. Holding Company Structures: Setting up holding company structures in jurisdictions with favorable tax laws can provide tax benefits for the corporation's global

operations.

5. Tax Havens and Offshore Jurisdictions: Some corporations may establish subsidiaries or conduct certain activities in low-tax or tax-free jurisdictions, commonly referred to as tax havens, to reduce tax liabilities.

6. Repatriation of Profits: Strategies for repatriating profits earned in foreign jurisdictions can be designed to minimize tax impact, considering factors like withholding taxes and foreign tax credits.

7. Intellectual Property (IP) Planning: Corporations can use IP planning to allocate profits to jurisdictions with more favorable IP tax regimes and lower effective tax rates.

8. Debt Financing: Properly structuring debt financing in international operations can optimize the use of interest deductions and reduce taxable income.

9. Base Erosion and Profit Shifting (BEPS): BEPS guidelines issued by the Organization for Economic Cooperation and Development (OECD) aim to prevent tax avoidance strategies and ensure fair taxation of multinational corporations.

10. Compliance and Reporting: Complying with tax regulations and reporting requirements in each country of operation is critical to avoid penalties and maintain a good reputation.

International tax planning for corporations requires a deep understanding of tax laws in multiple jurisdictions, as well as the ability to adapt to evolving tax regulations. It is essential for corporations to work with experienced tax advisors and legal professionals who specialize in international taxation to navigate the complexities and ensure compliance with all relevant tax laws.

Taxation of Pass-Through Entities (LLCs, Partnerships, etc.)

Pass-through entities, such as Limited Liability Companies (LLCs), partnerships, and S corporations, are business structures in which the business income "passes through" to the individual owners or members, who then report their share of the income on their personal tax returns. The business itself does not pay income tax at the entity level; instead, the tax liability is borne by the individual owners or members based on their share of the business's profits and losses.

Here are some key points about the taxation of pass-through entities:

1. Pass-Through Taxation: Pass-through entities are not subject to income tax at the entity level. Instead, the income, deductions, and credits of the business "pass through" to the owners, who report these items on their individual tax returns.

2. Flow-Through Income: The profits and losses of the pass-through entity flow through to the owners in proportion to their ownership interests. Each owner reports their share of the business income on their personal tax return, and it is taxed at their individual income tax rates.

3. Self-Employment Taxes: Owners of pass-through entities who are active participants in the business are typically subject to self-employment taxes, which include Social Security and Medicare taxes on their share

of the business income.

4. Deductions and Losses: Owners can deduct their share of the business's ordinary and necessary expenses on their personal tax returns. If the business incurs a net loss, the owners may be able to deduct the loss against other sources of income.

5. Basis and At-Risk Rules: Owners' basis and at-risk amounts in the pass-through entity affect their ability to deduct losses and claim certain tax benefits.

6. K-1 Forms: Pass-through entities provide each owner with a Schedule K-1, which reports their share of the business's income, deductions, and other items. Owners use the information on the K-1 to complete their personal tax returns.

7. Qualified Business Income Deduction: The Tax Cuts and Jobs Act (TCJA) introduced a new deduction for certain pass-through business income. The Qualified Business Income (QBI) deduction allows eligible taxpayers to deduct up to 20% of their share of qualified business income from a pass-through entity.

It's essential for owners of pass-through entities to understand their tax obligations and work with tax professionals to ensure proper reporting and compliance. The tax treatment of pass-through entities can vary based on the specific type of business, ownership structure, and individual circumstances, so seeking professional advice is crucial for maximizing tax benefits and minimizing tax liabilities.

Estates & Trusts Taxation

Estates and trusts taxation refers to the tax rules and regulations that apply to estates and trusts, which are legal entities created to manage and distribute assets and income for beneficiaries. The taxation of estates and trusts is separate from individual income tax and can be complex due to unique rules and reporting requirements. Here are some key points about estates and trusts taxation:

1. Income Taxation: Estates and trusts are subject to income tax on their taxable income, similar to individuals. They must report and pay taxes on any income earned from investments, rental properties, or other sources.

2. Tax Rates: The tax rates for estates and trusts are different from individual tax rates and can be more compressed. The tax brackets for estates and trusts are generally narrower, and higher tax rates may apply to lower levels of income.

3. Filing Requirements: Estates and trusts must file an annual income tax return, Form 1041, with the Internal Revenue Service (IRS). This return reports the income earned by the estate or trust and calculates the tax owed.

4. Deductions and Credits: Estates and trusts can deduct certain expenses related to the administration and management of the estate or trust. They can also claim credits for certain taxes paid and may be eligible for the Qualified Business Income (QBI) deduction if they have income from a qualified trade or business.

5. Distribution of Income: If the income earned by an

estate or trust is distributed to beneficiaries, the beneficiaries may be required to report that income on their individual tax returns.

6. Fiduciary Responsibility: The individual or entity responsible for managing the estate or trust, known as the fiduciary, has the duty to ensure that taxes are filed correctly and on time.

7. Estate Tax: In addition to income tax, there is a federal estate tax that applies to the value of large estates at the time of the owner's death. However, most estates are not subject to the federal estate tax due to the high exemption amount.

It's essential to work with a qualified tax professional, such as a tax attorney or accountant, to navigate the complexities of estates and trusts taxation. Proper tax planning and compliance can help maximize tax savings and ensure that the beneficiaries receive the intended assets and income from the estate or trust.

Estate Taxation and Filing Requirements

Estate taxation refers to the tax imposed on the value of an individual's estate upon their death. It is separate from income tax and is assessed on the total value of the assets owned by the deceased at the time of their death. Here are the key points about estate taxation and filing requirements:

1. Federal Estate Tax: The federal estate tax is a tax imposed by the U.S. government on the transfer of property from a deceased person's estate to their heirs. As of 2021, the federal estate tax applies to estates with a taxable value exceeding $11.7 million. This means that estates below this threshold are not subject to federal estate tax.

2. State Estate Tax: Some states also impose their own estate tax, which may have different exemption amounts and tax rates compared to the federal estate tax. Not all states have an estate tax, and the rules vary from state to state.

3. Filing Requirements: If an estate is subject to federal or state estate tax, an estate tax return must be filed with the appropriate tax authorities. For federal estate tax purposes, Form 706, United States Estate (and Generation-Skipping Transfer) Tax Return, is used to report the estate's assets and calculate the tax owed.

4. Valuation of Assets: The value of the assets in the estate is determined as of the date of the individual's death. Proper valuation of assets is crucial to ensure accurate reporting and calculation of the estate tax liability.

5. Estate Tax Exemptions and Deductions: Certain

deductions and exemptions are available to reduce the taxable value of the estate. For example, assets passed to a surviving spouse or qualified charitable organizations may be exempt from estate tax.

6. Portability: The concept of portability allows a surviving spouse to use any unused portion of their deceased spouse's estate tax exemption. This means that a surviving spouse may have a higher individual estate tax exemption if their spouse passed away and did not fully use their exemption.

7. Estate Tax Payment: The estate tax must be paid in cash, and the due date for payment is generally nine months after the date of the individual's death. However, an extension of time to file the estate tax return may be requested if needed.

Estate taxation can be complex, and the rules may change over time. It is essential to work with a qualified estate planning attorney or tax professional to ensure that the estate tax is properly calculated and that all available exemptions and deductions are applied. Proper estate planning can also help minimize the estate tax burden for beneficiaries.

Gift Taxation and Gift Tax Exclusions

Gift taxation refers to the tax imposed on the transfer of assets from one person (the donor) to another person (the recipient or donee) without any consideration or compensation in return. Here are the key points about gift taxation and gift tax exclusions:

1. Federal Gift Tax: The federal gift tax is a tax imposed by the U.S. government on the transfer of property as a gift during a person's lifetime. The purpose of the gift tax is to prevent individuals from avoiding the estate tax by giving away their assets before their death.

2. Annual Gift Tax Exclusion: The annual gift tax exclusion allows individuals to give a certain amount of money or property to another person each year without incurring any gift tax. As of 2021, the annual gift tax exclusion is $15,000 per recipient. This means that an individual can give up to $15,000 to as many individuals as they wish without having to file a gift tax return or pay any gift tax.

3. Lifetime Gift Tax Exemption: In addition to the annual gift tax exclusion, individuals have a lifetime gift tax exemption that allows them to give a certain total amount of gifts throughout their lifetime without incurring gift tax. As of 2021, the lifetime gift tax exemption is $11.7 million. This means that an individual can give gifts that exceed the annual exclusion but stay within the lifetime exemption without paying gift tax. However, any gifts that exceed the lifetime exemption will be subject to gift tax.

4. Gift Tax Returns: If a person makes gifts that exceed the

annual exclusion, they must file a gift tax return (Form 709) with the IRS. The gift tax return reports the gifts made during the tax year, and any tax owed is calculated based on the lifetime gift tax exemption.

5. Gift Splitting: Married couples have the option to split gifts, which means they can combine their annual exclusion amounts and give up to $30,000 per recipient without incurring gift tax. To do this, both spouses must consent to gift splitting on their gift tax returns.

6. Direct Payments: Certain payments made directly to educational institutions for tuition expenses or medical providers for medical expenses on behalf of another individual are not considered gifts and are not subject to the gift tax.

It is essential to keep track of gifts made throughout one's lifetime to ensure compliance with gift tax rules and to make informed decisions about gift-giving. Working with a qualified estate planning attorney or tax professional can help individuals understand the gift tax rules, maximize gift tax exclusions, and create a tax-efficient gifting strategy as part of their overall estate planning.

Taxation of Trusts and Trust Beneficiaries

The taxation of trusts and trust beneficiaries involves several key considerations. Here are the main points to understand:

1. Trust Taxation:
   - Revocable Trusts: Revocable trusts, also known as living trusts, are generally treated as "grantor trusts" for tax purposes. This means that the grantor (the person who created the trust) is considered the owner of the trust assets for income tax purposes, and the trust's income is reported on the grantor's individual tax return.
   - Irrevocable Trusts: Irrevocable trusts are separate taxable entities, and they may be subject to income tax at the trust level. Irrevocable trusts are subject to income tax rates that may be higher than individual tax rates, especially if the trust's income exceeds certain thresholds.

2. Distribution of Income:
   - Distributable Net Income (DNI): When an irrevocable trust distributes income to its beneficiaries, the income is taxed to the beneficiaries at their individual tax rates. The trust reports its distributable net income (DNI), which is the income available for distribution to beneficiaries, and the beneficiaries include

this income on their individual tax returns.

3. Taxation of Trust Beneficiaries:
   - Simple Trusts: Simple trusts are required to distribute all of their income to beneficiaries and do not accumulate income. The income distributed to beneficiaries is taxed to the beneficiaries at their individual tax rates.
   - Complex Trusts: Complex trusts have the option to accumulate income and distribute it in future years. The trust pays income tax on the income it retains, and the income distributed to beneficiaries is taxed to the beneficiaries.

4. Generation-Skipping Transfer (GST) Tax:
   - The GST tax is a tax imposed on certain transfers made to grandchildren or more remote descendants, as well as to certain unrelated individuals, such as non-family members who are more than 37.5 years younger than the donor. It is designed to prevent the avoidance of estate and gift taxes through generations.
   - Irrevocable trusts can be used as effective tools for GST tax planning, allowing wealth to be transferred to future generations while minimizing tax consequences.

5. Charitable Trusts:
   - Charitable trusts, such as charitable remainder trusts and charitable lead trusts, have unique tax considerations. The income and deductions associated with charitable trusts are subject to specific rules under the tax code.

6. State Income Tax:
   - State income tax treatment of trusts and trust beneficiaries varies from state to state. Some states have their own tax rules, which may

differ from federal tax rules.

Taxation of trusts and their beneficiaries can be complex and depend on various factors, including the type of trust, the nature of trust income, and the state in which the trust is established. It is essential to work with a qualified tax professional or estate planning attorney to navigate the tax implications of trusts and ensure compliance with relevant tax laws.

Estate Planning and Tax Minimization Strategies

Estate planning is the process of arranging and managing one's assets to ensure their efficient transfer to intended beneficiaries after death while minimizing tax liabilities. Here are some common estate planning and tax minimization strategies:

1. Wills and Trusts:
   - A well-drafted will allows individuals to specify how their assets will be distributed upon their death.
   - Trusts, such as revocable living trusts and irrevocable trusts, can be used to manage assets during one's lifetime and provide for their distribution after death, often while avoiding probate.
2. Lifetime Gifts:
   - Making gifts during one's lifetime can help reduce the size of the taxable estate and transfer assets to beneficiaries tax-free up to certain limits.
   - The annual gift tax exclusion allows individuals to gift a certain amount to each recipient without incurring gift tax.
3. Irrevocable Life Insurance Trust (ILIT):
   - An ILIT is a trust designed to own and manage life insurance policies outside of the insured's taxable estate.
   - The proceeds from the life insurance policy can

be used to provide liquidity to pay estate taxes or provide for beneficiaries.

4. Charitable Giving:
   - Donating to qualified charitable organizations can reduce the size of the taxable estate and may provide income tax deductions for the donor.

5. Qualified Personal Residence Trust (QPRT):
   - A QPRT allows individuals to transfer their residence or vacation home to an irrevocable trust while retaining the right to live in the property for a specified period.
   - After the trust term ends, the property passes to the beneficiaries without being included in the taxable estate.

6. Grantor Retained Annuity Trust (GRAT) and Grantor Retained Unitrust (GRUT):
   - GRAT and GRUT are irrevocable trusts that allow individuals to transfer assets to beneficiaries while retaining an annuity payment or unitrust interest for a specified term.
   - Any appreciation of the assets in excess of the IRS-prescribed interest rate goes to the beneficiaries free of gift tax.

7. Family Limited Partnerships (FLPs) and Limited Liability Companies (LLCs):
   - FLPs and LLCs can be used to transfer assets to family members while maintaining control over the assets.
   - Valuation discounts for lack of marketability and lack of control can reduce the taxable value of the transferred assets.

8. Generation-Skipping Transfer (GST) Tax Planning:
   - GST tax planning allows individuals to transfer assets to future generations while avoiding

estate and gift taxes at each generation.

9. Portability and Unified Credit:

- The concept of portability allows the surviving spouse to use any unused portion of the deceased spouse's federal estate tax exemption.
- The unified credit exempts a certain amount of assets from estate tax, which can be used during one's lifetime or at death.

It is essential to tailor estate planning strategies to individual circumstances and goals. Consulting with an experienced estate planning attorney and tax advisor can help individuals develop a comprehensive plan that addresses their specific needs and objectives while minimizing tax liabilities.

International Tax Law

International tax law deals with the tax implications of cross-border transactions and activities involving individuals, businesses, and other entities operating in multiple countries. It encompasses various tax laws, treaties, and regulations that govern the taxation of international transactions and the allocation of taxing rights between different jurisdictions. Here are some key aspects of international tax law:

1. Double Taxation Avoidance:
   - Many countries have tax treaties to avoid double taxation of income and ensure that taxpayers do not pay taxes on the same income in multiple jurisdictions.
   - These treaties typically provide rules for determining the residence of taxpayers, allocating taxing rights, and granting tax credits or exemptions to prevent double taxation.
2. Controlled Foreign Corporation (CFC) Rules:
   - CFC rules are designed to prevent taxpayers from deferring or avoiding tax by holding passive income in foreign subsidiaries with low tax rates.
   - Under CFC rules, certain income of foreign subsidiaries may be attributed to the parent company and subject to taxation in the home country.
3. Transfer Pricing:
   - Transfer pricing rules address the pricing of

transactions between related entities, such as subsidiaries of multinational corporations.
- The rules require that transactions between related parties be conducted at arm's length prices to prevent tax avoidance through transfer of profits to low-tax jurisdictions.

4. Taxation of Foreign Source Income:
   - Most countries tax their residents on worldwide income, but the treatment of foreign source income varies depending on the tax laws and treaties.
   - Some countries may offer foreign tax credits or provide exemptions for certain types of foreign income.

5. Tax Havens and Base Erosion and Profit Shifting (BEPS):
   - Tax havens are jurisdictions with low or no taxes that attract businesses seeking to reduce their tax liabilities.
   - BEPS refers to tax planning strategies used by multinational companies to shift profits to low-tax jurisdictions, resulting in reduced tax revenues for other countries.
   - The OECD's BEPS initiative aims to address these challenges and promote international tax cooperation.

6. Tax Treaties and Model Conventions:
   - Tax treaties are bilateral agreements between countries that allocate taxing rights and provide rules for resolving conflicts in taxation.
   - Many countries follow the OECD Model Tax Convention as a basis for negotiating tax treaties.

7. Foreign Account Tax Compliance Act (FATCA):
   - FATCA is a U.S. law that requires foreign financial institutions to report information

about U.S. account holders to the Internal Revenue Service (IRS).

- It aims to prevent tax evasion by U.S. citizens and residents with foreign financial accounts.

8. Country-by-Country Reporting (CbCR):

- CbCR is a reporting requirement for multinational enterprises to provide information on their operations, income, and taxes paid in each country where they operate.
- It helps tax authorities assess transfer pricing risks and profit shifting practices.

International tax law is complex and constantly evolving due to the dynamic nature of international commerce and global tax issues. Businesses and individuals engaged in international activities must carefully navigate these rules to comply with tax laws, avoid double taxation, and manage their tax liabilities effectively across multiple jurisdictions. Seeking advice from international tax experts and professionals is essential for sound tax planning and compliance in the global arena.

Principles of International Taxation

Principles of international taxation are fundamental guidelines and concepts that govern how countries tax cross-border transactions and income. These principles help to establish a fair and balanced system of taxation while avoiding double taxation and preventing tax evasion. Some key principles of international taxation include:

1. Residence Principle:
   - The residence principle determines the tax liability of individuals and businesses based on their residency status in a particular country.
   - Residents are generally subject to taxation on their worldwide income, while non-residents are taxed only on income earned within that country.
2. Source Principle:
   - The source principle determines the country that has the right to tax specific types of income based on where the income is generated or derived.
   - For example, income from immovable property is generally taxed in the country where the property is located, and income from business activities is taxed in the country where the activities take place.
3. Double Taxation Avoidance:
   - Double taxation avoidance is a fundamental principle to prevent the same income from being taxed twice in different countries.

- This is achieved through tax treaties and agreements that allocate taxing rights and provide mechanisms for granting relief from double taxation, such as tax credits or exemptions.

4. Transfer Pricing:
    - The transfer pricing principle ensures that transactions between related entities are conducted at arm's length prices, as if they were unrelated parties.
    - It aims to prevent multinational enterprises from artificially shifting profits to low-tax jurisdictions and avoiding taxation in higher-tax jurisdictions.

5. Tax Treaties:
    - Tax treaties are bilateral agreements between countries that provide rules for allocating taxing rights and resolving disputes regarding taxation of cross-border transactions and income.
    - They are based on the principles of residence and source and play a crucial role in harmonizing international tax rules.

6. Controlled Foreign Corporation (CFC) Rules:
    - CFC rules are designed to prevent taxpayers from deferring or avoiding tax by holding passive income in foreign subsidiaries with low tax rates.
    - Under CFC rules, certain income of foreign subsidiaries may be attributed to the parent company and subject to taxation in the home country.

7. Substance Over Form:
    - The substance over form principle emphasizes that the economic substance of a transaction or arrangement should prevail over its legal form

for tax purposes.

- Tax authorities may disregard transactions that lack economic substance or are solely designed to achieve tax benefits.

8. Tax Information Exchange and Transparency:
   - International tax cooperation involves the exchange of tax-related information among countries to combat tax evasion and promote transparency.
   - Initiatives such as the Common Reporting Standard (CRS) and the Foreign Account Tax Compliance Act (FATCA) facilitate the exchange of financial information between jurisdictions.

These principles, along with international tax laws and regulations, help guide tax planning and compliance for individuals and businesses engaged in cross-border activities. Understanding and adhering to these principles are essential for navigating the complexities of international taxation and ensuring tax compliance in a globalized world.

Double Taxation Treaties and Tax Planning

Double taxation treaties, also known as tax treaties or tax agreements, are bilateral agreements between two countries that aim to avoid double taxation and prevent tax evasion. These treaties establish the rules for taxing various types of income and transactions when they involve residents of both treaty countries. Double taxation treaties play a crucial role in international tax planning by providing clarity on tax liabilities and minimizing the overall tax burden for taxpayers engaged in cross-border activities.

Key aspects of double taxation treaties and their significance in tax planning include:

1. Taxation of Income:
   - Tax treaties allocate the taxing rights on different types of income, such as dividends, interest, royalties, and capital gains, between the two treaty countries.
   - This helps to prevent the same income from being taxed twice, once in the country where it is earned (source country) and again in the country of the taxpayer's residence.
2. Residence and Permanent Establishment:
   - Tax treaties define the criteria for determining an individual or a company's residence for tax purposes. It helps avoid situations where a taxpayer may be considered a resident in both

treaty countries and subject to double taxation on their worldwide income.

- Tax treaties also provide rules to determine when a business presence in one country constitutes a permanent establishment (PE) of a foreign company, triggering taxation in that country.

3. Withholding Tax Rates:
    - Tax treaties often reduce or eliminate the withholding tax rates on certain types of cross-border payments, such as dividends, interest, and royalties.
    - This can result in significant tax savings for taxpayers, as they can receive income from foreign sources at a lower or zero withholding tax rate.

4. Tax Credit or Exemption:
    - Tax treaties may provide for a tax credit or exemption to taxpayers in their country of residence for income that is already taxed in the source country.
    - This ensures that the taxpayer is not subject to double taxation on the same income.

5. Anti-Avoidance Provisions:
    - Many tax treaties include anti-avoidance provisions to prevent taxpayers from abusing the benefits of the treaty to engage in tax avoidance or treaty shopping.
    - Treaty shopping refers to the practice of routing transactions through a third country solely to take advantage of more favorable tax treaty provisions.

6. Mutual Agreement Procedure (MAP):
    - Tax treaties often include a mutual agreement procedure that allows taxpayers to resolve disputes or issues related to the application of

the treaty.
- Taxpayers can seek assistance from the competent authorities of both treaty countries to resolve any difficulties in interpreting or applying the treaty.

For businesses and individuals engaged in cross-border activities, tax treaties provide certainty and predictability in tax matters, which is essential for tax planning and decision-making. By taking advantage of the provisions in tax treaties, taxpayers can optimize their tax positions and minimize tax liabilities in a manner that complies with the tax laws of both treaty countries. However, it is essential to seek professional advice from tax experts and understand the specific provisions of the relevant tax treaty to ensure proper tax planning and compliance.

Controlled Foreign Corporations and Subpart F Rules

Controlled Foreign Corporations (CFCs) and Subpart F rules are important components of the U.S. tax system designed to prevent U.S. taxpayers from deferring taxes by holding investments in foreign corporations. These rules aim to discourage U.S. taxpayers from shifting income to low-tax or tax-haven jurisdictions through foreign corporate structures.

1. Controlled Foreign Corporations (CFCs):
   - A CFC is a foreign corporation in which U.S. shareholders own more than 50% of the total combined voting power of all classes of stock or more than 50% of the total value of the corporation's stock.
   - U.S. shareholders include U.S. individuals, corporations, partnerships, and certain trusts and estates.
   - When a foreign corporation meets the definition of a CFC, it becomes subject to the Subpart F rules.

2. Subpart F Rules:
   - The Subpart F rules, found in Subpart F of the U.S. Internal Revenue Code, require certain types of income earned by a CFC to be included in the taxable income of its U.S. shareholders, regardless of whether the income is distributed to them.
   - The goal of Subpart F rules is to prevent U.S.

taxpayers from deferring the recognition of certain types of passive income earned by their CFCs in low-tax jurisdictions.

3. Types of Income Covered by Subpart F:
   - Subpart F rules cover several types of passive income, including foreign base company income (FBCI), which consists of foreign personal holding company income (FPHCI) and foreign base company sales income (FBCSI).
   - FPHCI includes passive income such as dividends, interest, royalties, and rents.
   - FBCSI includes income from sales of goods purchased from related parties.

4. Exceptions and Limitations:
   - There are certain exceptions and limitations to the Subpart F rules to prevent double taxation and mitigate their impact on legitimate business operations.
   - For example, the high-tax exception allows certain income earned in high-tax jurisdictions to be excluded from Subpart F income.
   - Additionally, the de minimis rule excludes certain low levels of income from Subpart F inclusion.

5. Reporting and Compliance:
   - U.S. shareholders of CFCs must report their share of Subpart F income on their U.S. tax returns, even if they do not receive any actual distributions from the CFC.
   - Compliance with the Subpart F rules can be complex, and U.S. taxpayers with ownership interests in CFCs often seek the assistance of tax professionals to ensure proper reporting and compliance.

Overall, the Controlled Foreign Corporations and Subpart F rules are essential tools in preventing U.S. taxpayers from using foreign corporate structures to avoid or defer U.S. taxes on certain types of passive income. Understanding and complying with these rules is crucial for U.S. taxpayers with investments in foreign corporations to avoid potential tax liabilities and penalties.

Transfer Pricing and Base Erosion Profit Shifting (BEPS)

Transfer pricing and Base Erosion and Profit Shifting (BEPS) are related concepts in international taxation that aim to address the challenges posed by multinational enterprises (MNEs) in allocating profits and pricing transactions among their affiliated entities in different countries. These practices have the potential to erode the tax base of countries and result in the shifting of profits to low-tax jurisdictions.

1. Transfer Pricing:
   - Transfer pricing refers to the pricing of transactions between related parties, such as subsidiaries of the same multinational group, in different tax jurisdictions.
   - MNEs often engage in transfer pricing to determine the price at which goods, services, or intangible assets are transferred between their affiliated entities.
   - The objective of transfer pricing is to ensure that the prices set for these intra-group transactions are at arm's length, meaning they are comparable to what would have been charged between unrelated parties in similar transactions.

2. Arm's Length Principle:
   - The arm's length principle is a guiding principle in transfer pricing, endorsed by the Organisation for Economic Co-operation and

Development (OECD) and followed by many countries.

- Under the arm's length principle, the prices and terms of intra-group transactions should be determined as if they were conducted between unrelated parties in comparable circumstances.

3. Base Erosion and Profit Shifting (BEPS):

- BEPS refers to tax planning strategies used by MNEs to exploit gaps and mismatches in tax rules across different countries, resulting in the shifting of profits to low-tax or no-tax jurisdictions.
- The BEPS project was initiated by the OECD in 2013 to combat aggressive tax planning practices and ensure that multinational businesses pay their fair share of taxes in the countries where they operate.

4. OECD BEPS Action Plan:

- The OECD BEPS Action Plan consists of 15 specific actions that aim to address various aspects of BEPS and strengthen international tax rules to prevent profit shifting and tax avoidance.
- Some of the key actions include the introduction of country-by-country reporting, anti-tax treaty abuse provisions, and measures to curb harmful tax practices.

5. Implementation and Collaboration:

- Many countries have implemented BEPS recommendations and updated their tax laws to align with the new international standards.
- Collaboration among countries is essential to combat BEPS effectively, as profit shifting often involves cross-border transactions and complex structures.

6. Compliance and Enforcement:

- Multinational enterprises are now subject to increased scrutiny and reporting requirements to ensure compliance with transfer pricing rules and BEPS measures.
- Tax authorities are actively cooperating and exchanging information to detect and address potential instances of base erosion and profit shifting.

In summary, transfer pricing and BEPS are significant issues in international taxation that require ongoing attention and cooperation among countries to ensure a fair and effective tax system for both governments and multinational enterprises. The implementation of BEPS recommendations and the adherence to the arm's length principle in transfer pricing are critical steps in addressing tax avoidance and promoting transparency in the global economy.

Foreign Tax Credit and Foreign Earned Income Exclusion

Foreign Tax Credit and Foreign Earned Income Exclusion are two provisions in the United States tax code that aim to prevent double taxation of income for U.S. taxpayers who earn income abroad. These provisions allow eligible taxpayers to reduce their U.S. tax liability by either claiming a credit for foreign taxes paid or excluding a portion of their foreign earned income from U.S. taxation.

1. Foreign Tax Credit (FTC):
   - The Foreign Tax Credit allows U.S. taxpayers to offset the taxes they paid to a foreign country on their foreign-source income against their U.S. tax liability on the same income.
   - This credit is available for income that is subject to tax in both the U.S. and a foreign country, ensuring that taxpayers are not taxed twice on the same income.
   - To claim the FTC, taxpayers must file Form 1116 and meet certain eligibility requirements, including having foreign taxes that are legally owed and not refunded.
2. Foreign Earned Income Exclusion (FEIE):
   - The Foreign Earned Income Exclusion allows U.S. taxpayers who meet specific criteria to exclude a certain amount of their foreign earned income from U.S. taxation.
   - For tax year 2022, the maximum exclusion

amount is $108,700. This exclusion applies to wages, salaries, and self-employment income earned in a foreign country.

- To qualify for the FEIE, taxpayers must meet either the "Physical Presence Test" or the "Bona Fide Residence Test," which require them to spend a certain amount of time living and working abroad.

3. Choosing Between FTC and FEIE:

- Taxpayers who are eligible for both the Foreign Tax Credit and the Foreign Earned Income Exclusion can choose the option that provides the most beneficial tax outcome for their specific situation.
- In some cases, taxpayers may be able to utilize both provisions to reduce their overall U.S. tax liability.

4. Reporting Requirements:

- Claiming the Foreign Tax Credit or Foreign Earned Income Exclusion involves specific reporting requirements on the taxpayer's U.S. income tax return.
- It is essential to accurately report and document foreign income, foreign taxes paid, and any foreign tax credit or exclusion claimed to comply with the IRS regulations.

5. Limitations and Carryovers:

- The Foreign Tax Credit may be subject to certain limitations, such as the foreign tax credit limitation and the overall limitation on foreign taxes.
- Unused foreign tax credits can be carried back one year or carried forward ten years to offset U.S. tax on foreign-source income in future years.
- The Foreign Earned Income Exclusion is not a

credit; it is an exclusion from taxable income. Therefore, any income excluded under the FEIE cannot be used to claim the Foreign Tax Credit.

In conclusion, the Foreign Tax Credit and Foreign Earned Income Exclusion are essential provisions for U.S. taxpayers with foreign income. They play a crucial role in preventing double taxation and providing relief to individuals and businesses earning income abroad. Taxpayers must understand the eligibility criteria and reporting requirements to make informed decisions and maximize the benefits of these tax provisions.

Sales & Use Tax

Sales and Use Tax is a type of consumption tax levied by state and local governments in the United States. It is imposed on the sale of goods and certain services at the point of purchase and is typically collected by businesses on behalf of the government. Sales tax is a significant revenue source for state and local governments and is used to fund various public services and infrastructure projects.

Key concepts and features of Sales & Use Tax include:

1. Sales Tax:
   - Sales tax is levied on the retail sale of tangible personal property, such as clothing, electronics, furniture, and other goods.
   - The tax rate varies from state to state and can also differ within states, as local jurisdictions (e.g., counties and cities) may impose additional sales tax on top of the state rate.
   - Sales tax is typically calculated as a percentage of the purchase price of the goods or services.

2. Use Tax:
   - Use tax is a complementary tax to sales tax and is levied on the use, storage, or consumption of tangible personal property in a state where no sales tax was collected at the time of purchase.
   - It is designed to ensure that individuals and businesses do not evade sales tax by purchasing goods from out-of-state vendors and then using them in their home state.

3. Collection and Reporting:

- Businesses that sell goods subject to sales tax are required to collect the tax from customers at the time of sale.
- They are responsible for registering with the appropriate taxing authorities, calculating and collecting the correct amount of tax, and remitting the tax to the state or local government on a regular basis.
- Sales tax returns are typically filed monthly, quarterly, or annually, depending on the volume of sales and the state's regulations.

4. Exemptions and Taxability:
   - Some goods and services may be exempt from sales tax, depending on the state's tax laws. Examples of exempt items may include groceries, prescription medications, and certain medical services.
   - Different states have different rules regarding the taxability of specific items, so businesses must be aware of their state's tax laws to correctly apply sales tax.

5. Marketplace Facilitator Laws:
   - In response to the growth of online marketplaces, many states have enacted marketplace facilitator laws. These laws require online platforms like Amazon and eBay to collect and remit sales tax on behalf of their third-party sellers.

6. Economic Nexus and Remote Sellers:
   - With the Supreme Court's decision in South Dakota v. Wayfair in 2018, states can now require remote sellers (those without a physical presence in the state) to collect and remit sales tax based on economic nexus criteria, such as a certain amount of sales or transactions in the state.

Sales & Use Tax is a complex and evolving area of tax law. Businesses and individuals must stay informed about changes in tax rates, exemptions, and reporting requirements to ensure compliance with state and local tax laws. Additionally, the increasing prominence of e-commerce and online marketplaces has brought new challenges and considerations for sales tax collection and remittance.

Basics of Sales Tax and Nexus

Sales tax is a consumption tax imposed on the sale of goods and, in some cases, services. It is typically collected by businesses at the point of sale and remitted to the appropriate state or local government. The tax rate may vary depending on the jurisdiction and the type of goods or services being sold.

Nexus refers to the connection or presence that a business must have in a state or locality to be subject to sales tax laws. In the context of sales tax, nexus determines whether a business is required to collect and remit sales tax to a particular state or local jurisdiction.

Key points about sales tax and nexus include:

1. Physical Presence Nexus: Traditionally, businesses were required to have a physical presence in a state, such as a brick-and-mortar store, warehouse, or office, to establish nexus and be subject to sales tax in that state.
2. Economic Nexus: In recent years, the concept of economic nexus has gained prominence due to changes in state laws and the Supreme Court decision in South Dakota v. Wayfair. Economic nexus is based on a business's level of economic activity in a state, such as the volume of sales or the number of transactions conducted in that state.
3. Thresholds for Economic Nexus: States have different thresholds for economic nexus, and businesses that exceed these thresholds are considered to have nexus and are required to collect and remit sales tax. Thresholds may be based on a certain amount of sales

revenue or a minimum number of transactions in a state.

4. Marketplace Facilitator Laws: Some states have enacted marketplace facilitator laws, which require online marketplaces like Amazon and eBay to collect and remit sales tax on behalf of their third-party sellers. This relieves individual sellers from the burden of collecting and remitting sales tax.

5. Streamlined Sales Tax Agreement: Some states participate in the Streamlined Sales Tax Agreement (SSTA), a cooperative effort among states to simplify sales tax collection and administration. Businesses that voluntarily comply with the SSTA's rules may receive certain benefits, such as reduced compliance burdens.

6. Sales Tax Exemptions: Certain goods and services may be exempt from sales tax, depending on state and local laws. Examples of exempt items include groceries, prescription medications, and certain medical services.

7. Use Tax: In cases where sales tax was not collected at the time of purchase, individuals and businesses may be required to pay use tax on the use, storage, or consumption of taxable goods in their home state.

Understanding the basics of sales tax and nexus is crucial for businesses engaged in interstate commerce to ensure compliance with state and local tax laws. It is essential to keep abreast of changes in tax laws and regulations, especially as the landscape of sales tax collection continues to evolve with the growth of e-commerce and cross-border transactions.

E-commerce and State Sales Tax Issues

E-commerce has revolutionized the way goods and services are bought and sold, and it has also presented challenges for state sales tax collection. State sales tax issues related to e-commerce primarily revolve around the concept of nexus and the collection of sales tax from online retailers.

1. Nexus and Economic Presence: As mentioned earlier, nexus is the connection or presence that a business must have in a state to be subject to that state's sales tax laws. In the context of e-commerce, the traditional physical presence standard has been expanded to include economic presence. This means that even if an online retailer does not have a physical presence in a state, it may still have nexus and be required to collect and remit sales tax based on its level of economic activity in that state.

2. Wayfair Decision: The 2018 Supreme Court decision in South Dakota v. Wayfair overturned the physical presence standard and upheld South Dakota's economic nexus law. This decision opened the door for other states to enact similar economic nexus laws, allowing them to require out-of-state sellers, including e-commerce retailers, to collect and remit sales tax if they meet certain economic thresholds.

3. Marketplace Facilitator Laws: Many states have enacted marketplace facilitator laws that shift the responsibility for collecting and remitting sales tax from individual

sellers to the online marketplace platform (e.g., Amazon, eBay) that facilitates the sale. Under these laws, the marketplace platform is considered the seller for purposes of sales tax collection and is required to collect and remit sales tax on behalf of its third-party sellers.

4. Voluntary Collection Agreements: Some states have entered into voluntary collection agreements (VCAs) with large e-commerce retailers, allowing the retailers to collect and remit sales tax voluntarily, even if they do not have a physical or economic presence in the state. This is seen as a way to simplify tax compliance for both businesses and consumers.

5. Complexity and Compliance Burden: E-commerce retailers that sell to customers in multiple states face the challenge of complying with the sales tax laws of each state, as each state has its own tax rates, exemptions, and rules. This complexity can be a burden for smaller e-commerce businesses that do not have the resources to manage multiple state tax filings.

6. Use Tax Reporting: In some cases, states require consumers to self-report and remit use tax on their online purchases if sales tax was not collected at the time of purchase. However, use tax compliance by individual consumers is often low, leading to potential revenue losses for states.

Overall, e-commerce has prompted states to adapt their sales tax laws to address the challenges of collecting tax from online retailers and to level the playing field between brick-and-mortar stores and online sellers. As a result, e-commerce businesses need to stay informed about the evolving state tax laws and ensure compliance with sales tax requirements to avoid potential penalties and legal issues. Seeking the advice of tax professionals and using automated sales tax compliance software can help e-commerce retailers navigate the complexities of state sales tax collection and reporting.

Use Tax and Reporting Requirements

Use tax is a complementary tax to sales tax and is imposed on the use, storage, or consumption of tangible personal property or taxable services that were purchased without sales tax being collected. It is typically levied by the state where the property or service is used, rather than where it was purchased.

Use tax is designed to prevent tax avoidance and ensure that taxpayers pay the appropriate amount of tax, regardless of whether the purchase was made in-state or out-of-state. It applies to situations where sales tax was not collected at the time of purchase, such as when an individual or business buys goods online from a seller that does not have a physical presence in the buyer's state.

Reporting Requirements: The reporting and remittance of use tax are typically the responsibility of the consumer or purchaser, rather than the seller. In most states, individuals and businesses are required to report their use tax liability on their state income tax returns or on a separate use tax return.

If an individual or business owes use tax, they must calculate the tax based on the purchase price of the goods or services and the applicable tax rate in their state. Some states provide a use tax rate that is the same as the state's sales tax rate, while others may have a different rate for use tax.

States vary in their enforcement and collection of use tax. Some states have robust use tax compliance programs, while others rely on voluntary compliance by taxpayers to report and remit use tax.

Enforcement: Despite the legal obligation to report and remit use tax, compliance rates are often low. Many individuals and businesses are either unaware of their use tax obligations or choose not to comply voluntarily. As a result, states may attempt to increase compliance through various means, such as information sharing with other states and using data analytics to identify potential non-compliant taxpayers.

It is important for individuals and businesses to understand their use tax obligations and ensure compliance with state laws. Failing to report and remit use tax when required can result in penalties and interest on unpaid taxes. Seeking guidance from tax professionals and using automated tax software can help ensure accurate reporting and remittance of use tax.

Property Tax

Property tax is a tax levied on the value of real property, such as land, buildings, and improvements, that is owned by individuals, businesses, or other entities. It is a major source of revenue for local governments, including cities, counties, school districts, and special districts. Property tax funds public services and infrastructure, such as schools, parks, roads, and public safety.

Key Aspects of Property Tax:

1. Property Assessment: Local assessors determine the value of the property for tax purposes. This value is usually based on the fair market value of the property, which is the price at which it would sell in an open market.

2. Mill Levy or Tax Rate: The tax rate, often expressed in mills (one mill is equal to one-tenth of a cent), is applied to the assessed value of the property to calculate the property tax amount. For example, if the tax rate is 100 mills and the assessed value of the property is $100,000, the property tax would be $100,000 x (100/1,000) = $10,000.

3. Exemptions and Deductions: Some jurisdictions offer property tax exemptions or deductions for certain types of property or property owners, such as homestead exemptions for primary residences or exemptions for properties owned by nonprofit organizations.

4. Tax Collection: Property taxes are typically collected by the local government, and the revenue is used to fund local services and programs. In some areas, property taxes may be collected by a county or state agency on

behalf of local governments.

5. Assessment Appeals: Property owners have the right to appeal the assessed value of their property if they believe it is incorrect or unfair. The appeals process allows property owners to present evidence to support their claim for a lower assessed value.

6. Tax Lien and Delinquency: Failure to pay property taxes can result in a tax lien being placed on the property. In extreme cases of non-payment, the local government may seize and sell the property to recover the unpaid taxes.

Property tax laws and regulations vary by jurisdiction, and each locality may have its own rules regarding assessment methods, tax rates, and exemptions. Property owners should be aware of their rights and obligations related to property taxes and stay informed about changes in local tax laws. It is advisable for property owners to review their property tax assessments annually and consider appealing if they believe their property has been overvalued. Additionally, seeking advice from tax professionals can help property owners understand their property tax obligations and identify potential tax-saving opportunities.

Assessment and Valuation
of Real Property

Assessment and valuation of real property is a critical process in determining the property's worth for property tax purposes. Local government assessors are responsible for evaluating the value of properties within their jurisdiction to determine the amount of property tax that property owners are required to pay. The assessment and valuation process involves several key steps:

1. Data Collection: Assessors gather information about the property, including its location, size, construction details, amenities, and any improvements or changes made to the property.
2. Property Inspection: Assessors may conduct physical inspections of the property to verify the information collected and assess its condition and features.
3. Market Analysis: Assessors consider the real estate market conditions, recent sales of similar properties in the area (comparables), and other market data to determine the property's fair market value.
4. Valuation Methods: There are various valuation methods used to determine the value of real property, including the sales comparison approach, income approach, and cost approach.
   - Sales Comparison Approach: This method compares the property to recently sold similar properties (comparables) in the area to estimate its value.
   - Income Approach: The income approach is

used for income-generating properties, such as rental properties or commercial buildings. It assesses the property's value based on its potential income and the rate of return expected by investors.

- Cost Approach: This method estimates the property's value based on the cost to replace or reproduce the property, considering depreciation and obsolescence.

5. Assessment Notices: After completing the valuation, the assessor notifies property owners of their property's assessed value through assessment notices or property tax bills.

6. Appeals Process: Property owners have the right to appeal their property's assessed value if they believe it is inaccurate or unfair. The appeals process allows property owners to present evidence to support their claim for a lower assessed value.

Assessment and valuation methods can vary by jurisdiction, and local tax laws and regulations govern the process. It is essential for property owners to understand how their property's value is determined and to review their property tax assessments regularly to ensure accuracy. Consulting with a tax professional or appraiser can be helpful in understanding the assessment and valuation process and identifying any potential errors or discrepancies.

Property Tax Exemptions and Appeals

Property tax exemptions are special privileges granted to certain properties that relieve them from paying some or all property taxes. These exemptions are typically provided by local governments and vary from one jurisdiction to another. Common types of property tax exemptions include:

1. Homestead Exemption: This exemption is often available to homeowners who use their property as their primary residence. It provides a reduction in the assessed value of the property, resulting in lower property taxes.
2. Senior Citizen Exemption: Some jurisdictions offer property tax exemptions for senior citizens, usually those above a certain age, to help ease the tax burden on fixed-income individuals.
3. Disabled Veteran Exemption: Veterans with disabilities may be eligible for property tax exemptions as a way to recognize their service and sacrifice.
4. Charitable and Nonprofit Organizations: Properties owned by charitable and nonprofit organizations may be exempt from property taxes if they are used for qualifying purposes, such as religious, educational, or charitable activities.
5. Agricultural Exemption: Agricultural properties that are actively used for farming or ranching purposes may qualify for property tax exemptions.

Appealing a property tax assessment is an option for property owners who believe their property has been overvalued or inaccurately assessed. The appeals process varies by jurisdiction, but it generally involves the following steps:

1. Review the Assessment: Property owners should review their property tax assessment carefully to understand how the value was determined.
2. Gather Evidence: Property owners should collect evidence to support their claim that the assessed value is incorrect. This may include recent property appraisals, comparable sales data, or evidence of any property defects or damages.
3. File an Appeal: Property owners must file a formal appeal with the appropriate tax assessment appeal board or agency within the specified time frame. The appeal typically requires a written statement explaining the reasons for the appeal and supporting evidence.
4. Attend a Hearing: In some cases, property owners may have the opportunity to present their case in a hearing before the appeal board. They can present their evidence and arguments to support their claim for a lower assessed value.
5. Await Decision: The appeal board will review the evidence and make a decision on the appeal. If the appeal is successful, the property's assessed value may be adjusted, resulting in a lower property tax bill.

It is essential for property owners to understand the deadlines and procedures for property tax exemptions and appeals in their local jurisdiction. Consulting with a tax professional or real estate attorney can be beneficial in navigating the process and increasing the likelihood of a successful appeal.

Tax Audits and Disputes

Tax audits and disputes occur when tax authorities, such as the Internal Revenue Service (IRS) in the United States, examine a taxpayer's financial records and tax returns to verify the accuracy and completeness of reported income and deductions. Audits can be stressful for taxpayers, but being prepared and understanding the process can help alleviate some of the anxiety.

Here are the key points to know about tax audits and disputes:

1. Types of Audits: There are different types of tax audits, including correspondence audits conducted by mail, office audits where taxpayers meet with IRS agents, and field audits where the IRS visits the taxpayer's home or business.

2. Triggers for Audits: Tax audits can be triggered by various factors, such as inconsistencies in reported income, high deductions compared to income level, involvement in certain high-risk activities, or random selection.

3. Records and Documentation: Keeping accurate and organized records is essential for supporting the information reported on tax returns. Taxpayers should maintain records of income, expenses, and supporting documents for at least three to seven years, depending on the item.

4. Responding to the Audit: If selected for an audit, taxpayers should respond promptly and provide the requested information to the IRS. Being cooperative and responsive can help the audit process go smoothly.

5. Hiring Representation: Taxpayers have the right to

represent themselves in an audit, but they can also choose to hire a tax professional, such as a tax attorney or certified public accountant (CPA), to represent them during the audit.

6. Audit Outcomes: After the audit, the IRS may accept the tax return as filed or propose changes. Taxpayers have the right to appeal if they disagree with the proposed changes.

7. Tax Disputes and Appeals: Taxpayers who disagree with the IRS's findings can pursue a formal appeal process, such as requesting a meeting with an IRS manager or filing an appeal with the IRS Office of Appeals.

8. Tax Court: If the dispute remains unresolved after the appeal, taxpayers have the option to bring their case to the United States Tax Court or a federal district court.

9. Penalties and Interest: Depending on the circumstances, taxpayers may face penalties and interest for underpayment of taxes or failure to comply with tax laws.

It's crucial for taxpayers to be honest and accurate in their tax reporting to minimize the likelihood of an audit and avoid potential penalties. In case of an audit, being prepared, providing complete documentation, and seeking professional advice can help ensure a smoother process and a fair resolution.

Tax Audits and IRS Examination Process

Tax audits and IRS examination processes are conducted to ensure that taxpayers are complying with tax laws and accurately reporting their income, deductions, and credits. The Internal Revenue Service (IRS) conducts audits to verify the information reported on tax returns and to identify any discrepancies or potential issues. Here are the key points to understand about tax audits and the IRS examination process:

1. Selection for Audit: Tax returns can be selected for an audit through various methods, including random selection, computerized screening for potential errors or inconsistencies, and information matching with third-party data (e.g., W-2s, 1099s).

2. Types of Audits: The IRS conducts different types of audits, including correspondence audits, office audits, and field audits. Correspondence audits are conducted through mail, while office and field audits involve in-person meetings with IRS agents.

3. Notification: If selected for an audit, taxpayers receive an official notification from the IRS, usually by mail, stating the reason for the audit and the specific items or areas under examination.

4. Recordkeeping: Taxpayers should keep accurate and organized records of their income, deductions, and credits. Good recordkeeping is essential for supporting the information reported on tax returns in case of an audit.

5. Gathering Documentation: When audited, taxpayers are required to provide documentation and evidence to support the amounts reported on their tax returns. This may include receipts, invoices, bank statements, and other financial records.

6. Representation: Taxpayers have the right to represent themselves during an audit or to have a tax professional, such as a tax attorney or CPA, represent them. Having representation can help navigate the audit process and protect taxpayers' rights.

7. Audit Process: The audit process involves a review of the specific items in question. IRS agents may ask questions, request additional documentation, and examine financial records to ensure accuracy and compliance with tax laws.

8. Audit Outcomes: After the audit, the IRS may make no changes to the tax return, propose adjustments, or request additional tax owed. Taxpayers have the right to appeal proposed changes if they disagree.

9. Appeals Process: Taxpayers who disagree with the audit findings can appeal within the IRS through the Office of Appeals. The appeals process provides an opportunity to resolve disputes without going to court.

10. Tax Court: If the appeal is unsuccessful or if the taxpayer chooses not to appeal, they may have the option to bring the case to the United States Tax Court or a federal district court.

It's essential for taxpayers to cooperate with the IRS during an audit and provide requested documentation in a timely manner. By keeping accurate records and seeking professional advice if needed, taxpayers can navigate the audit process more effectively and ensure compliance with tax laws.

Tax Litigation and Court Procedures

Tax litigation refers to the legal process of resolving tax disputes between taxpayers and tax authorities, such as the Internal Revenue Service (IRS) in the United States. When taxpayers and the IRS cannot reach a resolution through the audit and appeals process, the dispute may proceed to tax court or other judicial proceedings. Here are the key aspects of tax litigation and court procedures:

1. Tax Court: The United States Tax Court is a specialized federal court that hears tax-related cases. Taxpayers can bring their cases to Tax Court without first paying the disputed tax, which sets it apart from other courts. Tax Court judges have expertise in tax law, and cases are often decided based on the application of tax laws and regulations.

2. Other Courts: Tax disputes can also be litigated in other federal courts, such as the U.S. District Court or the U.S. Court of Federal Claims. Taxpayers may have different options for pursuing their cases in different courts, depending on the circumstances of the dispute.

3. Jurisdiction: Courts have specific jurisdiction over tax cases, and taxpayers must ensure that they file their cases in the appropriate court with the proper jurisdiction.

4. Commencement of Litigation: Tax litigation typically begins when the taxpayer files a petition in the appropriate court to challenge the IRS's proposed adjustments or tax assessments.

5. Discovery: During tax litigation, both parties have the

opportunity to engage in the discovery process to gather evidence and information relevant to the case.

6. Pre-Trial Motions: Before the trial, both parties may file pre-trial motions to address procedural issues or seek rulings on specific legal matters.
7. Trial: The trial is the main phase of tax litigation, during which both parties present their arguments, evidence, and witnesses before the court.
8. Burden of Proof: In tax litigation, the burden of proof generally falls on the taxpayer to show that the IRS's proposed adjustments or assessments are incorrect.
9. Rulings and Decisions: After considering the evidence and arguments presented during the trial, the court will issue its ruling or decision. The court's decision may uphold the IRS's position, partially agree with the taxpayer, or rule entirely in favor of the taxpayer.
10. Appeals: If either party is dissatisfied with the court's decision, they may have the option to appeal the case to a higher court.

Tax litigation can be a complex and time-consuming process, and it's important for taxpayers to have legal representation by tax attorneys or other professionals experienced in tax law. An understanding of the relevant tax laws, court procedures, and strategies for presenting a case is crucial to achieving a favorable outcome in tax litigation.

Appeals and Taxpayer Representation

Appeals play a crucial role in the tax dispute resolution process, providing taxpayers with an opportunity to challenge adverse decisions made by tax authorities. When taxpayers disagree with the outcome of an audit, assessment, or other tax-related matter, they have the right to appeal the decision through a formal process. Here are the key aspects of appeals and taxpayer representation:

1. Administrative Appeal: In many tax jurisdictions, taxpayers are required to exhaust administrative remedies by filing an appeal with the tax authority before seeking judicial review. Administrative appeals allow taxpayers to present their case to a different office within the tax authority, often known as the Appeals Division or Office of Appeals. Appeals officers are independent and impartial, and their role is to review the case and attempt to facilitate a fair and impartial resolution.

2. Grounds for Appeal: Taxpayers can appeal decisions based on various grounds, such as errors in tax assessments, incorrect application of tax laws, or disputes over tax liability. They may also challenge penalties and interest imposed by tax authorities.

3. Notice of Deficiency: In some jurisdictions, taxpayers receive a Notice of Deficiency (also known as a Statutory Notice of Deficiency or 90-Day Letter) before a formal assessment is made. The notice informs the taxpayer of the proposed tax deficiency and provides a specific timeframe within which to file a petition with the tax

court if they disagree.

4. Petition to Tax Court: If the taxpayer disagrees with the outcome of the administrative appeal or receives a Notice of Deficiency, they may file a petition with the tax court. Tax court petitions provide taxpayers with the opportunity to litigate their case before a judicial forum.

5. Representation: Taxpayers have the right to represent themselves in appeals and tax court proceedings. However, due to the complexity of tax laws and procedures, many taxpayers choose to be represented by tax professionals, such as tax attorneys, certified public accountants (CPAs), or enrolled agents (EAs). Tax professionals can provide valuable guidance, advocacy, and expertise throughout the appeals process.

6. Settlement Negotiations: During the appeals process, settlement negotiations between the taxpayer and the tax authority may occur. Appeals officers often act as mediators to facilitate discussions and find a mutually acceptable resolution to the dispute.

7. Taxpayer Advocate Service (TAS): In some jurisdictions, there is a Taxpayer Advocate Service or a similar entity that offers assistance to taxpayers experiencing significant hardships or facing challenges in resolving tax problems. The TAS provides an independent review of taxpayers' concerns and works to ensure that their rights are protected.

8. Mediation: In certain cases, taxpayers and tax authorities may opt for mediation as an alternative dispute resolution method. Mediation involves a neutral third party facilitating discussions between the parties to reach a resolution without going to court.

The appeals process provides an important avenue for taxpayers to seek redress and have their tax disputes fairly and impartially evaluated. Timely and appropriate representation by tax professionals can significantly enhance a taxpayer's chances of achieving a favorable outcome in the appeals process.

Tax Ethics and Professional Responsibility

Tax ethics and professional responsibility are crucial aspects of tax practice, as tax professionals play a significant role in advising clients on tax matters and ensuring compliance with tax laws. Adherence to ethical standards is essential to maintain the integrity of the tax system and build public trust in tax professionals. Here are some key considerations related to tax ethics and professional responsibility:

1. Confidentiality: Tax professionals must maintain strict confidentiality regarding their clients' tax information. They should not disclose any confidential information to third parties without the client's consent, except as required by law.

2. Competence: Tax professionals are expected to possess the necessary knowledge and skills to provide competent tax advice and services to their clients. They should stay up-to-date with changes in tax laws and regulations and be aware of current tax planning strategies.

3. Conflict of Interest: Tax professionals should avoid conflicts of interest that may compromise their objectivity and independence. They should not engage in any activities or relationships that could adversely affect their ability to provide unbiased advice to their clients.

4. Accuracy and Diligence: Tax professionals have a duty to be diligent in their work and strive for accuracy in

preparing tax returns and providing tax advice. They should exercise due care and reasonable judgment to avoid errors or omissions.

5. Tax Avoidance vs. Tax Evasion: Tax professionals should distinguish between legal tax planning (tax avoidance) and illegal tax evasion. While tax planning is acceptable and often encouraged, tax evasion is a criminal offense that involves willful attempts to evade taxes by fraudulent means.

6. Disclosure and Transparency: Tax professionals should be transparent with their clients about the tax implications of various transactions and activities. They should provide clear and honest explanations of tax consequences to enable clients to make informed decisions.

7. Representation before Tax Authorities: When representing clients before tax authorities, tax professionals must adhere to ethical standards and present accurate and truthful information. They should not make false or misleading statements to tax authorities.

8. Avoiding Abusive Tax Shelters: Tax professionals should refrain from promoting or participating in abusive tax shelters or tax schemes designed to create artificial tax deductions or credits.

9. Reporting Professional Misconduct: Tax professionals have an obligation to report suspected instances of professional misconduct by colleagues or others in the tax profession.

10. Continuing Education: Tax professionals should engage in continuous learning and professional development to stay abreast of changes in tax laws, regulations, and best practices.

Professional organizations and licensing bodies often have codes of ethics that govern the behavior and conduct of tax professionals. Violations of ethical standards can lead to disciplinary actions, loss of professional licenses, and reputational damage.

By adhering to high ethical standards and maintaining professional responsibility, tax professionals contribute to a fair and transparent tax system and build trust with their clients and the broader public.

Ethics in Tax Practice

Ethics in tax practice refers to the moral principles and standards that tax professionals must adhere to when providing tax advice and services to clients. Ethics are essential in maintaining the integrity of the tax system and ensuring that taxpayers receive accurate and unbiased advice. Here are some key aspects of ethics in tax practice:

1. Integrity: Tax professionals must act with honesty and integrity in all their interactions with clients, tax authorities, and other stakeholders. They should avoid any actions that could compromise their objectivity or reputation.

2. Confidentiality: Tax professionals have a duty to maintain the confidentiality of their clients' tax information. They should not disclose any confidential information without the client's consent, except as required by law.

3. Competence: Tax professionals should possess the necessary knowledge and skills to provide competent tax advice and services. They should stay current with changes in tax laws and regulations to ensure they can effectively serve their clients' needs.

4. Avoiding Conflicts of Interest: Tax professionals should avoid situations that may create conflicts of interest and could impact their ability to provide impartial advice to their clients. They should prioritize their clients' interests above their own.

5. Accuracy and Diligence: Tax professionals should exercise due care and diligence in preparing tax returns

and providing tax advice. They should strive for accuracy and avoid errors or omissions in their work.

6. Avoiding Unethical Practices: Tax professionals should not engage in unethical or illegal practices, such as promoting tax evasion, participating in abusive tax schemes, or providing false information to tax authorities.

7. Transparency and Disclosure: Tax professionals should be transparent with their clients about the tax implications of various transactions and activities. They should disclose any potential risks or uncertainties in the tax advice they provide.

8. Compliance with Laws and Regulations: Tax professionals have a responsibility to comply with all applicable tax laws, regulations, and professional standards in their practice.

9. Reporting Professional Misconduct: Tax professionals should report any suspected instances of professional misconduct by colleagues or others in the tax profession.

10. Continuing Education: Tax professionals should engage in ongoing professional development to stay informed about changes in tax laws and regulations and to enhance their skills and knowledge.

Professional organizations and licensing bodies often have codes of ethics that govern the conduct of tax professionals. Violations of ethical standards can result in disciplinary actions, loss of professional licenses, and damage to the tax professional's reputation.

By upholding high ethical standards, tax professionals not only fulfill their duties to their clients but also contribute to the overall fairness and trustworthiness of the tax system.

Avoiding Tax Fraud and Abusive Tax Schemes

Avoiding tax fraud and abusive tax schemes is essential for tax professionals to maintain their integrity and protect their clients from legal and financial consequences. Here are some key steps tax professionals can take to avoid involvement in tax fraud and abusive tax schemes:

1. Know the Tax Laws: Tax professionals must have a thorough understanding of tax laws and regulations to ensure that they provide accurate and compliant advice to their clients.
2. Avoid Promoting Tax Evasion: Tax professionals should never advise or encourage clients to engage in tax evasion, which involves intentionally underreporting income or overstating deductions to reduce tax liability.
3. Avoid Abusive Tax Shelters: Tax professionals should steer clear of promoting or participating in abusive tax shelters or schemes that are designed to generate artificial tax losses or deductions.
4. Identify Red Flags: Tax professionals should be vigilant in identifying potential red flags in their clients' tax returns or transactions that may indicate tax fraud or abusive practices.
5. Report Suspected Fraud: If tax professionals encounter suspicious activities that may indicate tax fraud or abusive tax schemes, they have a legal obligation to report them to the appropriate authorities.
6. Perform Due Diligence: Tax professionals should

thoroughly research and analyze any tax strategies or transactions before advising clients to ensure their legitimacy and compliance with tax laws.

7. Disclose Risks: If tax professionals are aware of potential risks or uncertainties associated with a tax strategy, they must disclose these to their clients to ensure informed decision-making.

8. Stay Informed: Tax laws and regulations are subject to frequent changes, so tax professionals must stay up-to-date with the latest developments to avoid inadvertently providing outdated or inaccurate advice.

9. Use Reliable Sources: Tax professionals should rely on credible sources, such as official tax authorities and reputable tax publications, for information and guidance.

10. Professional Ethics: Upholding ethical standards is paramount for tax professionals to maintain their credibility and protect their clients from potential harm.

11. Continual Education: Tax professionals should engage in ongoing education and professional development to enhance their knowledge and skills, ensuring they can provide the best possible advice to their clients.

Tax professionals should be aware that engaging in tax fraud or abusive tax schemes can lead to severe legal consequences, including civil and criminal penalties, loss of professional licenses, and damage to their reputation. By prioritizing compliance with tax laws and adhering to ethical standards, tax professionals can help ensure the integrity of the tax system and protect their clients' interests.

Tax Policy and Social Justice

Tax policy plays a crucial role in promoting social justice and addressing economic inequality within a society. Social justice refers to the fair and equitable distribution of resources, opportunities, and benefits among all members of a community, regardless of their socioeconomic status, race, gender, or other factors. Tax policy can be a powerful tool for achieving social justice goals by ensuring that the burden of taxation is distributed fairly and that government revenues are used to fund programs and services that benefit the most vulnerable and marginalized members of society.

Some key aspects of tax policy that contribute to social justice include:

1. Progressive Taxation: A progressive tax system is one in which higher-income individuals pay a higher percentage of their income in taxes compared to lower-income individuals. This approach recognizes that those with higher incomes can afford to contribute more to the public coffers, while lower-income individuals may struggle to meet basic needs.

2. Targeted Tax Credits and Deductions: Tax credits and deductions can be designed to provide targeted relief to specific groups, such as low-income families, caregivers, and individuals with disabilities. These tax incentives can help alleviate financial burdens and promote economic mobility for vulnerable populations.

3. Wealth and Inheritance Taxes: Implementing wealth and inheritance taxes can help address wealth inequality by taxing the assets and estates of the

wealthiest individuals and families. These taxes can be structured to prevent the concentration of wealth and promote a more equitable distribution of resources.

4. Corporate Taxation: Fair and effective corporate taxation can ensure that businesses contribute their fair share to society. Closing tax loopholes and preventing tax avoidance by multinational corporations can help ensure that corporations contribute to the communities where they operate.

5. Use of Tax Revenue: How tax revenue is utilized is a crucial aspect of promoting social justice. Investments in education, healthcare, affordable housing, social services, and other essential public goods can help reduce disparities and create opportunities for all members of society.

6. Transparent and Inclusive Policy-Making: Involving diverse stakeholders in the development of tax policies and ensuring transparency in the tax system can promote accountability and prevent policies that disproportionately benefit the wealthy or powerful.

7. Consideration of Intersectionality: Tax policy should consider the unique challenges faced by individuals who experience multiple forms of discrimination, such as people of color, LGBTQ+ individuals, and individuals with disabilities. Understanding the intersectionality of these identities can inform tax policies that address the specific needs and barriers faced by these communities.

By incorporating principles of social justice into tax policy, governments can create a more equitable and inclusive society, where all individuals have the opportunity to thrive. However, achieving social justice through tax policy can be complex, requiring thoughtful analysis, political will, and ongoing evaluation of the policy's impact on various segments of society.

Progressive Taxation and Economic Inequality

Progressive taxation is a tax system in which the tax rate increases as the taxable income or wealth of individuals or entities increases. It is often used as a tool to address economic inequality by redistributing wealth and resources from higher-income individuals to lower-income individuals. The progressive tax system is based on the principle of ability-to-pay, which means that those who earn higher incomes can afford to pay a higher percentage of their income in taxes, while those with lower incomes pay a lower percentage.

Key features and impacts of progressive taxation on economic inequality include:

1. Redistribution of Income: Progressive taxation helps to redistribute income from high-income individuals to low-income individuals. The higher tax rates on the wealthy contribute to funding social programs and services that benefit the less privileged members of society.

2. Reduced Wealth Inequality: By taxing higher-income individuals at higher rates, progressive taxation can help reduce wealth inequality. This is particularly important in societies where wealth is highly concentrated among a small percentage of the population.

3. Poverty Alleviation: Progressive taxation can be used to fund social safety net programs, such as welfare, food

assistance, and housing subsidies, which can help lift people out of poverty and provide a basic standard of living.

4. Social Mobility: Progressive taxation can contribute to greater social mobility by providing resources for education, job training, and other programs that help individuals move up the economic ladder.

5. Counteracting Regressive Taxes: Regressive taxes, such as sales taxes, tend to burden lower-income individuals disproportionately. Progressive taxation can help offset the regressive impact of these taxes and create a more equitable tax system overall.

6. Political Debate: The design and implementation of progressive taxation can be a subject of political debate. Some argue that higher taxes on the wealthy may discourage investment and economic growth, while others believe that the benefits of a more equal society outweigh these concerns.

7. Tax Avoidance and Evasion: High-income individuals may use various strategies to minimize their tax liability, including tax shelters and offshore accounts. Enforcing progressive tax policies and closing loopholes is essential to ensuring their effectiveness.

While progressive taxation can be an effective tool in addressing economic inequality, it is not without challenges. Careful consideration must be given to setting tax brackets and rates to balance the goal of redistribution with economic growth and efficiency. Additionally, international tax competition and globalization can create challenges in implementing progressive tax policies on a global scale.

Overall, progressive taxation is a fundamental aspect of many tax systems aimed at promoting social justice and reducing economic inequality. It continues to be a topic of ongoing discussion and debate as societies seek to strike a balance between fiscal responsibility, economic growth, and equitable distribution of resources.

Tax Incentives and Social Policy

Tax incentives are provisions in the tax code that are designed to encourage specific behaviors or activities deemed beneficial to society or the economy. These incentives are used as tools to promote social policy objectives and influence individual and corporate behavior. They are typically offered in the form of deductions, credits, exemptions, or preferential tax rates.

Tax incentives can be used to achieve various social policy goals, such as:

1. Promoting Economic Growth: Tax incentives can stimulate economic activity by encouraging investment, job creation, and business expansion. For example, tax credits for research and development expenses or investment in certain industries can spur innovation and economic growth.

2. Encouraging Savings and Investment: Tax-advantaged retirement accounts and investment vehicles, such as Individual Retirement Accounts (IRAs) and 401(k) plans, incentivize individuals to save for the future and invest in financial markets.

3. Fostering Homeownership: Tax deductions for mortgage interest and property taxes incentivize homeownership and can make housing more affordable for many individuals and families.

4. Supporting Education: Tax credits and deductions for educational expenses, such as the Lifetime Learning Credit and the Tuition and Fees Deduction, can help ease the financial burden of pursuing higher education.

5. Promoting Energy Efficiency and Sustainability: Tax

credits for the purchase of energy-efficient appliances or renewable energy systems incentivize individuals and businesses to adopt environmentally friendly practices.

6. Supporting Charitable Giving: Tax deductions for charitable donations encourage philanthropy and support nonprofit organizations that provide essential services to communities.

7. Addressing Social Issues: Tax incentives can also be used to address specific social issues, such as childcare expenses, affordable housing, and healthcare costs.

While tax incentives can be effective in promoting desired behaviors and achieving social policy objectives, they also have some limitations and challenges. For example:

- Complexity: The proliferation of tax incentives can lead to a complex and convoluted tax code, making it challenging for taxpayers to navigate and understand their tax obligations fully.
- Equity Concerns: Some argue that tax incentives disproportionately benefit higher-income individuals and corporations, potentially exacerbating income inequality.
- Revenue Loss: Tax incentives result in reduced government revenue, which may impact funding for critical public services and social programs.

As a result, policymakers must carefully consider the design and implementation of tax incentives to ensure they achieve their intended goals while maintaining fairness and fiscal responsibility. Regular evaluation and review of tax incentives are essential to assess their effectiveness and make any necessary adjustments to align with changing societal needs and priorities.

Taxation and Environmental Considerations

Taxation can be used as a tool to address environmental considerations and promote sustainable practices. By incorporating environmental objectives into the tax system, governments can incentivize environmentally friendly behavior, discourage harmful practices, and fund environmental initiatives. Some ways taxation can be used to address environmental concerns include:

1. Carbon Taxes: Carbon taxes are levied on the carbon content of fossil fuels, which encourages businesses and individuals to reduce their carbon emissions and transition to cleaner energy sources. The revenue generated from carbon taxes can be used to support renewable energy projects and other climate initiatives.

2. Pollution Taxes: Taxes on pollutants can discourage industrial activities that generate harmful emissions or waste. By imposing higher taxes on polluting industries, governments can promote cleaner and more sustainable practices.

3. Green Tax Credits and Deductions: Tax credits and deductions can be provided to individuals and businesses that engage in environmentally friendly activities, such as installing solar panels or using energy-efficient appliances.

4. Waste Disposal Taxes: Taxes on waste disposal can encourage recycling and waste reduction efforts while discouraging the generation of non-recyclable or hazardous waste.

5. Incentives for Sustainable Transportation: Tax

incentives can be offered to encourage the adoption of electric vehicles or other eco-friendly transportation options, reducing greenhouse gas emissions from the transportation sector.

6. Land Use and Conservation Taxes: Taxes on land use and development can incentivize conservation and protect natural habitats. Landowners may receive tax breaks for preserving ecologically sensitive areas.

7. Tax on Single-Use Plastics: Some jurisdictions have implemented taxes on single-use plastics to reduce plastic waste and promote more sustainable packaging alternatives.

8. Environmental Offsets: Tax credits or deductions can be offered to businesses or individuals that invest in projects that offset their environmental impact, such as reforestation efforts or renewable energy projects.

9. Environmental Impact Assessments: Taxation can be linked to the environmental impact of certain projects, with higher taxes imposed on activities that have significant environmental consequences.

10. Funds for Environmental Programs: Revenue generated from environmental taxes can be earmarked for funding environmental protection and conservation programs.

While using taxation as a tool to address environmental considerations can be effective, it is essential to strike a balance between environmental objectives and economic growth. Careful consideration and consultation with stakeholders are necessary to ensure that tax policies are both environmentally effective and economically feasible. Moreover, coordination and cooperation among countries are crucial in addressing global environmental challenges.

Current Trends and Emerging Issues in Tax Law

Current trends and emerging issues in tax law are shaped by various factors, including technological advancements, globalization, changing economic landscapes, and societal demands. Some of the key trends and issues in tax law include:

1. Digital Economy Taxation: The rise of the digital economy has led to challenges in taxing digital transactions and cross-border e-commerce. Countries are exploring new taxation models to ensure that multinational tech companies pay their fair share of taxes in the countries where they operate.

2. Base Erosion and Profit Shifting (BEPS): BEPS refers to tax planning strategies used by multinational corporations to shift profits to low-tax jurisdictions, reducing their overall tax liability. Governments are implementing measures to counteract BEPS and ensure that multinational companies pay taxes where economic activities occur.

3. Tax Transparency and Reporting: There is growing demand for tax transparency, with increased reporting requirements for businesses to disclose their tax information. Tax authorities and international organizations are working to combat tax evasion and promote transparency in tax matters.

4. Environmental Taxation: As environmental concerns become more prominent, governments are using taxation as a means to encourage sustainable practices,

such as carbon taxes, green tax incentives, and taxes on single-use plastics.

5. Cryptocurrency Taxation: The rapid growth of cryptocurrencies has created challenges in taxing virtual currencies. Governments are developing regulations and guidelines for taxing cryptocurrency transactions and holdings.

6. Tax Incentives for Economic Recovery: In response to the COVID-19 pandemic, many countries have implemented tax incentives and relief measures to support businesses and individuals during economic downturns.

7. International Tax Cooperation: Countries are increasingly cooperating to address tax evasion, information exchange, and treaty disputes. Efforts like the OECD's Inclusive Framework on BEPS promote collaboration in tax matters.

8. Taxation of the Sharing Economy: The sharing economy, including platforms like Uber and Airbnb, presents tax challenges due to the decentralized nature of transactions. Tax authorities are adapting tax regulations to capture income from sharing economy activities.

9. Wealth and Inequality Taxation: In response to growing income inequality, some jurisdictions are considering wealth taxes or higher tax rates for high-income individuals to address wealth disparities.

10. Environmental, Social, and Governance (ESG) Reporting: Investors and stakeholders are increasingly demanding ESG reporting from companies, including tax practices that align with sustainable and ethical standards.

11. Tax Policy in Post-Pandemic Recovery: As economies recover from the pandemic, governments are reassessing their tax policies to support economic growth, job creation, and fiscal stability.

12. Automation and Tax Compliance: Automation and digital tools are transforming tax compliance processes, making tax reporting more efficient and reducing the risk of errors.

These trends and emerging issues in tax law reflect the evolving nature of the global economy and the need to balance revenue generation with social and environmental responsibilities. Tax professionals must stay informed about these developments to navigate the complexities of the modern tax landscape effectively.

Digital Economy and Tax Challenges

The digital economy has transformed the way business is conducted, with the widespread use of technology, online platforms, and e-commerce. While the digital economy has brought numerous benefits, it has also presented unique tax challenges for governments worldwide. Some of the key tax challenges in the digital economy include:

1. Nexus and Permanent Establishment: Traditional tax rules were designed for brick-and-mortar businesses with a physical presence in a jurisdiction. In the digital economy, businesses can operate across borders without a physical presence, raising questions about where they should be taxed and whether they have a sufficient nexus or permanent establishment in a particular country.

2. Cross-Border Transactions: Digital transactions can easily occur across borders, making it difficult for tax authorities to track and tax these transactions accurately. As a result, taxing digital goods and services, such as software downloads and online advertising, becomes a challenge.

3. Transfer Pricing: Multinational digital companies may use complex transfer pricing arrangements to shift profits to low-tax jurisdictions. Ensuring that multinational corporations allocate profits appropriately between different countries has become a significant issue for tax authorities.

4. Data and User Privacy: Tax authorities may need access to data from digital platforms to determine the tax

liability of companies operating in the digital economy. However, access to user data raises concerns about privacy and data protection.

5. Determining Value Creation: In the digital economy, value creation often involves intangible assets, such as user data and intellectual property. Taxing the value created in digital transactions can be complex and may require new approaches to measure and attribute value.

6. Platform Business Models: Platforms that connect buyers and sellers, such as e-commerce marketplaces and ride-sharing services, may have unique tax implications. Determining the appropriate tax treatment for platform providers and users can be challenging.

7. Double Taxation and Tax Competition: The lack of global consensus on taxing the digital economy can lead to double taxation or tax competition among countries, creating uncertainty for businesses and potential conflicts between jurisdictions.

8. VAT/GST Challenges: Cross-border digital sales can lead to challenges in applying Value Added Tax (VAT) or Goods and Services Tax (GST) to digital products and services, especially when multiple jurisdictions are involved.

To address these challenges, countries and international organizations are actively working on developing new tax rules and policies. The Organization for Economic Cooperation and Development (OECD) and the G20 have been leading efforts through the Base Erosion and Profit Shifting (BEPS) project and the Digital Economy Taxation initiatives to establish common frameworks for taxing the digital economy.

In conclusion, the digital economy's rapid growth has brought about significant tax challenges, requiring innovative and coordinated efforts among governments to develop fair and effective taxation rules for digital transactions and activities. As technology continues to evolve, tax professionals and policymakers will need to stay proactive in adapting tax systems to ensure they remain relevant and equitable in the digital age.

Cryptocurrency and Taxation

Cryptocurrency has become increasingly popular in recent years, and its tax treatment has been a topic of interest and concern for tax authorities worldwide. The taxation of cryptocurrencies can vary depending on the jurisdiction, the nature of the cryptocurrency transactions, and the taxpayer's specific circumstances. Here are some key aspects of cryptocurrency taxation:

1. Classification: Different countries may classify cryptocurrencies differently for tax purposes. Some treat them as currencies, while others view them as property or assets. The classification can have significant implications for how cryptocurrencies are taxed.

2. Capital Gains Tax: In many jurisdictions, cryptocurrencies are treated as assets, and any gains or losses from their sale or exchange are subject to capital gains tax. The tax rate may vary based on the holding period, with short-term gains typically taxed at higher rates than long-term gains.

3. Income Tax: For individuals who receive cryptocurrencies as payment for goods or services, the value of the cryptocurrency at the time of receipt may be considered taxable income. Businesses that accept cryptocurrencies as payment may also need to account for the value received in their income.

4. Reporting Requirements: Taxpayers who engage in cryptocurrency transactions may be required to report their activities to tax authorities, including

details of transactions, gains, and losses. Failure to report accurately could result in penalties or other consequences.

5. Mining and Staking: Cryptocurrency miners and stakers, who validate transactions and add blocks to the blockchain, may be subject to taxation on the rewards they receive for their efforts.

6. Gift and Inheritance Tax: Transfers of cryptocurrencies as gifts or inheritance may trigger tax implications, depending on the jurisdiction's gift and inheritance tax laws.

7. Use Tax: Some jurisdictions impose taxes on purchases made with cryptocurrencies, similar to sales tax or value-added tax (VAT).

8. Airdrops and Forks: Cryptocurrency airdrops (free distributions) and forks (blockchain splits) can create complex tax situations, and their treatment may vary depending on local regulations.

Given the complexities and evolving nature of cryptocurrency taxation, individuals and businesses involved in cryptocurrency transactions are advised to seek guidance from tax professionals who are knowledgeable in this area. Staying compliant with tax obligations and reporting requirements is essential to avoid potential penalties or legal issues related to cryptocurrency taxation. As the cryptocurrency space continues to evolve, tax authorities are also likely to refine their policies and regulations to address the challenges posed by this rapidly growing digital asset class.

Tax Implications of COVID-19 Relief Measures

The COVID-19 pandemic led to widespread economic disruption, and governments around the world implemented various relief measures to support individuals and businesses during this challenging time. These relief measures can have significant tax implications, and taxpayers should be aware of how they may affect their tax obligations. Here are some common tax implications of COVID-19 relief measures:

1. Economic Impact Payments (Stimulus Checks): Many governments provided direct cash payments to individuals to help alleviate financial strain. In general, these stimulus payments are not taxable income and do not need to be reported on tax returns.

2. Unemployment Benefits: Unemployment benefits increased significantly during the pandemic as a result of higher unemployment rates. While unemployment benefits are taxable income, taxpayers have the option to have taxes withheld from their benefits to avoid a large tax bill when filing their returns.

3. Paycheck Protection Program (PPP) Loans: Businesses that received forgivable PPP loans may be eligible for tax-free forgiveness of the loan proceeds if the funds were used for qualified expenses like payroll, rent, and utilities. However, the expenses paid with the forgiven PPP loan funds are not tax-deductible, creating a unique tax situation for business owners.

4. Employee Retention Credit (ERC): The ERC was

introduced to encourage businesses to retain employees during the pandemic. Eligible employers can claim a refundable tax credit for a portion of qualified wages paid to employees. The ERC provides a potential tax benefit to businesses.

5. Tax Deadline Extensions: Some jurisdictions extended tax filing and payment deadlines in response to the pandemic. Taxpayers should be aware of these deadline extensions to avoid penalties for late filing or payment.

6. Remote Work and Nexus: With many employees working remotely during the pandemic, there may be tax implications related to state income taxes and potential changes in tax nexus for businesses.

7. Charitable Contributions: Many governments incentivized charitable giving by providing enhanced tax deductions for donations to qualifying charities.

8. Retirement Account Distributions: Early withdrawal penalties for retirement account distributions were waived for COVID-19-related hardships, and some jurisdictions allowed for tax-deferred repayment of distributions.

It is essential for taxpayers to understand the specific relief measures implemented in their jurisdiction and how they impact their individual or business tax situations. Consulting with a tax professional can help navigate the complexities of the tax implications related to COVID-19 relief measures and ensure compliance with applicable tax laws.

Conclusion

In conclusion, "Mastering Taxation: A Comprehensive Guide to Tax Law and Practice" provides a thorough exploration of the complex and ever-evolving world of tax law. Throughout this comprehensive guide, readers have delved into various aspects of taxation, from its historical development to its current trends and emerging issues. The book has shed light on the foundational principles of tax law, the different types of taxes, and the various legal and ethical considerations that tax professionals must navigate.

The significance of taxation in society cannot be overstated. Taxes play a crucial role in funding public services, supporting social policies, and promoting economic growth. Understanding tax laws and regulations is essential for individuals, businesses, and governments to comply with their tax obligations while optimizing their financial positions.

The guide has covered a wide range of tax topics, including individual income taxation, corporate taxation, estate and trust taxation, international taxation, sales and use tax, property tax, and the implications of digital economy and cryptocurrency on tax matters. It has also highlighted the role of tax policy in addressing economic inequality and social justice issues.

Mastering taxation requires a comprehensive knowledge of tax laws, the ability to navigate complex legal provisions, and a commitment to ethical tax practice. Tax professionals must stay updated on the latest tax developments and be prepared to address the challenges and opportunities presented by the ever-changing tax landscape.

Throughout this journey, the guide has emphasized the importance of ethical conduct in tax practice, promoting social responsibility, and upholding the principles of fairness and equity in taxation. Tax professionals have a critical role to play in ensuring compliance with tax laws, protecting taxpayer rights, and contributing to the greater good of society through responsible tax planning and reporting.

As the world of taxation continues to evolve, mastering tax law and practice will remain an ongoing pursuit. Tax professionals must remain vigilant in adapting to new regulations, addressing emerging tax issues, and staying informed about global tax developments.

"Mastering Taxation: A Comprehensive Guide to Tax Law and Practice" aims to equip readers with the knowledge and skills necessary to navigate the complexities of tax law and contribute positively to the field of taxation. Whether readers are tax practitioners, business owners, or individuals seeking to understand their tax obligations better, this guide serves as a valuable resource to deepen their understanding of taxation.

In conclusion, the study of taxation is not just about numbers and regulations; it is a multifaceted discipline that intersects with economics, law, social policy, and ethics. By mastering taxation, individuals and professionals can make informed decisions, comply with tax laws, and contribute to a fair and equitable tax system that benefits society as a whole.

www.ingramcontent.com/pod-product-compliance
Lightning Source LLC
Chambersburg PA
CBHW062323290526
45794CB00005B/1868